# The Art of Breathing:
## Abiding in Christ

## By Gina Roes

D1158886

PRESS

*The Art of Breathing*
*Abiding in Christ*
by Gina Roes

Printed in the United States of America

ISBN 9781609575717

www.xulonpress.com

RENEE-

MAY ABIDING BECOME

YOUR NEW NORMAL!

GINA ROES

JOHN 15:5

For Beth
Thanks for showing me that I could blow out the dragon.

# Table of Contents

# Introduction

While following Jesus and abiding in Him go together, they are not the same thing. Following focuses on action, like obedience and service. Abiding emphasizes resting, remaining, living within. As we grow in Christ, we begin by following Him, just like His disciples. When Jesus called the Twelve, He bid them to follow Him. But as His ministry on earth began to draw to an end, He asked them to abide in Him like a branch abides in a vine. He asks us to do the same. We follow Him, but then we must grow to a place of abiding. The way we train children in the lessons of right and wrong, following Christ teaches us the basics of how we function in our Christian walk. We ask, "What would Jesus do?" and we focus on obedience to His word. But at some point we must move from milk to meat. We must allow obedience to flow from something rather than depend on it to get us to something.

I have never met anyone who feels they have too much joy or peace.

Does fruit come from striving or abiding? Does a branch strive to produce fruit or does it come from a healthy connection to the vine? Can we really have love, joy, peace, patience, kindness, goodness, gentleness, faithfulness, and self-control by trying harder? If so, wouldn't we have already tried by now?

So what about the church-attending evangelical who just can't seem to find the abundance part of the abundant life? What about the man in Sunday school class whose marriage is falling apart, who tithes and takes communion, but believes the Bible does not work for him they way it seems to be working for others? Or the Christian who can't forgive herself for the past and is trying desperately to find the right "formula" to win God's favor. In her head, of course, she knows this is not the truth. But her heart's experience won't allow her to live according to what her head knows. She feels trapped and, therefore, she goes through the motions of church and faith but her heart still feels broken. It is God's desire to reach them with the depth of the Gospel and see their hearts transformed, even if their circumstances never change.

Life on this side of Eden is not what we hoped for. It is not what we were made for. Something is missing. As we abide in Christ, we offer Him our hearts. He, in turn, offers His heart. We point to Him. He points to us. We give Him our pain. He heals and restores us to wholeness. We give our sin. He gives His forgiveness. We give our lives. He gives His life. We breathe out ourselves and inhale His presence, a fluid motion of abiding. This is the abundant life. This is the art of breathing.

This book is divided into four sections: Naming, Owning, Surrendering, and Living. This project began as a fairytale that I have included as the preface. Questions at the end of each chapter are there to help you go deeper and can be used as a guide for journaling or for small group discussion.

As you engage in this journey, I pray you will encounter the depth of the Good News and the abundance of life that has been offered to you. God speed on your journey.

# A Real Life Fairy Tale

Once upon a time, there lived a little girl who was badly injured. Bruises and welts covered her little soul from the battles she had endured. Then one day, her heart went numb as she chose not to feel anymore. She tried to find shelter from her explosive surroundings and ran to a place called Isolation. Here, there was no more conflict. There was also no comfort. In her attempts to comfort herself, she became buried beneath the heavy, burdensome rocks of her own efforts to cope and was left for dead. It seemed no one could hear her faint cries because in Isolation, there was no one who cared.

I learned that someone from Heaven, however, was listening. Seeing the injuries from the beginning, he told me she must be in Isolation. It was the only predictable place. He vowed that he would not give up until he not only found her, but healed her as well. He, himself, would bring comfort to her. But this hero faced two obstacles. The first had to do with his name. His name was the Wind, the one who makes breathing possible. To a hurting little girl, however, Wind offers little comfort. He knew she would need someone's arms to hold her. Therefore, he enrolled me to help. His second obstacle was the mighty Dragon that guarded the rock pile that covered the child. No one could reach her until the Dragon was overthrown.

The little girl had long ceased to be afraid of the Dragon. It had been there so long that it seemed normal. As strange as it sounds, she relied on its presence for a taste of consistency, in that every day was always the same. She could always count on the Dragon to keep her trapped. She had given up trying to get out and resigned herself to live under the rocks forever. After all, at least she couldn't hurt anymore. Her senses were numb.

The days crept by and boredom began to set in. She made a few attempts to crawl out, but the pain was too much, and the Dragon would breathe fire on her and hurt her even more. She gave up trying. She started to miss the days when life seemed exciting and fun. After the injuries, however, nothing was fun anymore. Isolation was her only choice.

The Wind from Heaven wept to see her there. He also saw the Dragon and was not afraid. In fact, the enormous size of the Dragon made him all the more determined to save the child. He would not let the Dragon win. I admired his courage and strength and wanted to help him.

He pulled me aside and began to teach me his plan to save the hurting little girl. "She needs help soon," he said, "because the numbness is wearing off. You can't have injuries that long without eventually feeling the pain, and she is afraid the pain will kill her. When she is rescued," he continued, "she will begin to hurt deeply. Her wounds will be exposed to the air. When that happens, it will be overwhelming."

"I'm ready," I said.

Then, with wisdom and compassion he said, "Your mission is to gently uncover her and carry her back to a place that I have created just for her. It's called Safety. There we will be able to enjoy nature together, and write songs and tell stories as often as we like. But we must hurry. She doesn't yet know her name."

"Her name?" I asked, "What is her name?"

"I will show you," he replied.

I felt excited to find this child and carry out my assignment.

As we walked toward Isolation together, darkness settled around us. I did not like the cold stillness. Isolation seemed to be a picture of frozen darkness. "Why would a child choose to live here?" I wondered aloud.

The Wind explained that Isolation feels much better than the place from which she came. "It is cold here," he said, "but she escaped a land that is very hot, where explosions always cause injuries. This little girl is lucky to have made it out alive. Many people come here as they attempt to escape other lands." He was not surprised when we found her there. It was the first place he looked.

As we approached the last mountain before the rock pile that covered the broken little girl, my anticipation grew. Anxiety gripped me. Thoughts tumbled around my mind. "What will happen next? How damaged is she? Will I know what to do to help? What will happen to this One from Heaven?" He seemed to know so much about the little girl. I was growing fond of his company and hoped he would continue to be with me after she was rescued.

We crested the top of the mountain, and I found myself eye-to-eye with the Dragon. I had no idea how huge it would be. Its feet were down in the valley, and its head was level with the mountain on which I was standing. The gigantic beast delighted in keeping the child trapped. I felt helpless.

The Dragon saw us approaching and began to stir. Smoke billowed from its nostrils; it aimed its smoldering nose at us to snuff us out and to keep us from the child. I was paralyzed. I had never seen a Dragon before, and I couldn't believe my eyes. "How is one supposed to conquer a Dragon?" I thought.

"Are you ready?" my heavenly friend asked.

"I am," I said, looking for the little girl in the distant pile of rocks.

As I focused on the rocks, the Dragon turned its head toward me. Suddenly, fire exploded from its mouth, and I had nowhere to go. I panicked and waited for the pain. But there was none. The flames did not even touch me. How could this be? Then I saw the answer. The Wind was blowing the flames out. I watched in amazement as every last flame was extinguished. I stood in awe, and I was filled with a new kind of love for this warrior Wind. He knew just what to do. I watched the battle unfold, and at each turn, my hero disarmed his enemy.

The Dragon became even angrier and fought harder. The flames came from embers deep within the Dragon that had been smoldering there for a long time - long before the little girl was even born. The Dragon clearly hated the Wind. The Wind came near to me and told me that no matter what happened I was to rescue the little girl as we had planned. I was confused. Of course I would do that. Why would he tell me that?

And then it happened. The Wind disappeared. The evidence of him vanished all together. I was left alone in this windless place called Isolation with an angry Dragon to overcome and an injured child to rescue. How could he do this? How could he leave me here like this? How could he enroll me to help and then disappear?

I scrambled for the pile of rocks. The Dragon, angrier than ever, chased after me. I knew I could not escape such a huge beast, and I was running out of options. Something inside of me caused me to stop. I turned around as a wall of fire blasted in my direction. As if by instinct, I blew with all my might.

The Wind came out of me and blew out the Dragon's fire.

I did not realize that while I had breathed in the Wind's company, he had entered me and made his home inside of me. Now I could stop the Dragon. But could I prevent the Dragon from hurting the little girl? Was there enough Wind inside me for both of us? Surely he would not have promised such a thing if he were not going to provide it.

Desperate to keep the child trapped, the Dragon seethed with hatred, billowing fire out of its every pore to prevent me from reaching the rocks. I turned, blew as hard as I could, and knocked the Dragon down. Amazed, I stood stunned for a moment. I didn't know I had it in me. I remembered what the Wind had told me to do. I needed to get the little girl out gently. I needed to get her out of Isolation before the Dragon woke up. But would it wake up? The Dragon cannot live anywhere else. It can't live where there is Wind. Wind blows it out.

Slowly, I began to uncover the wounded little girl, but she was afraid to see me. I was a stranger. The usual Dragon sounds that had been her constant companion were silenced, at least for the moment, and my voice spoke instead. She didn't know how to hear tender words, only harsh words. I spoke tenderly anyway. As I moved the rocks, her raw, damaged soul was revealed. I cried as I looked at all the wounds. How could anyone do this to a child? Some of the injuries were from her own choices as she had tried to comfort herself in Isolation, but it really didn't matter to me where the damage came from; she needed comfort. I picked her up (which hurt her very much) and began to carry her out. Crying, because she didn't understand where we were going, she begged, "Please let me stay under the rocks, out of the painful air."

Gently, I replied, "You do not understand now, but one day you will see that the big world is full of adventure, not just scary things." I also told her that the Wind and I would be with her for the rest of her life. She was never going to be alone again.

I took the little girl to Safety as I was instructed. When we arrived, the landscape was incredible. Bright and beautiful, the warmth of the sun chased away the left over chill in our bodies from being in Isolation. But then I noticed that the landscape looked vaguely familiar. Somehow, it seemed to resemble Isolation. I noticed the rock pile, now empty, in the distance. Then I saw the charred grass where the Dragon had been. My heart began to race as my eyes scanned the horizon and there, like a small dot against the sky, was the Dragon…waiting. Even so, my fear dissipated. The Dragon looked so small now. Yes, this was the place where Isolation had been. It was the exact same dirt. But it was also different … or maybe I was different.

Then an understanding washed over me. I realized something that I hadn't noticed before. When I experienced the Wind's power, he had given me new eyes. I was seeing my surroundings with brand new eyes. What used to be dark was now bright. What used to be cold was now welcoming. What used to be overwhelming was now a tiny dot against the horizon. What used to be the sole defense against the Dragon was now an empty pile of rocks, an empty tomb. It all suddenly made sense to me. The little girl, however, had trouble seeing the difference between Isolation and Safety. To her it looked much the same.

"That is why I am here," I told her. "I will see the difference for you. When you feel like you are back in the same place, I will use my new eyes to see things as they really are."

The little girl took it all in. She felt lighter. A burden was lifted. She no longer needed to figure out how to defeat the Dragon. She could be small. She could be safe. She could be free. It was now time to really live. It was now okay to feel.

As we took in the view, the little girl began to warm up. Having been in cold Isolation for so long, it felt good to be warm.

I was relieved that the rescue had gone well but missed the intense fellowship of my companion. Then one day, as I sat in Safety with the little girl, the Wind met us there. With a gentleness that can only be true in fairy tales, he looked deeply into the little girl's eyes and offered her a name, her real name. "Your name is, and has always been, Precious. It is time to live your name."

Then, unexpectedly, the Wind turned to me. "I have a name for you as well," he said. "Your name is Trustworthy. I give you stewardship over Precious, which is no small thing. I entrust to you what cost me everything."

He taught me how to care for the child. "Keep her warm," he said, "and hug and kiss the injuries often." And then he spoke the words I'll never forget.

"If you ever wonder where I am," he said, "just breathe."

# Naming...

- designation, terming, definition, identification

*"In Jewish thought, a name is not merely an arbitrary designation, a random combination of sounds. The name conveys the nature and essence of the thing named. It represents the history and reputation of the thing named." Tracey R. Rich*

*"To write a story is an act of naming." Madeline L'Engle*

To give something a name is to call forth its place. A child carries the name of the parents, designating the child belongs with the parents. A doctor gives a name, a diagnosis; indentifying the role an illness is playing in the body. Naming gives answers to questions like: Who am I? Where am I? Why am I here? What went wrong? And how does it get better? The act of naming pulls us into reality—into the way things really are, into who we really are. What is your name?

# 1
# Once Upon A Time:
## *Naming Our Role in the Story*

*"The storyteller is a storyteller because the
storyteller cares about truth, searching for truth,
expressing truth, sharing truth. But that cannot be
done unless we know our craft." Madeline L'Engle*

*"Remember, God is still writing." Dan Allender*

Once upon a time God created man and woman from
the dust of the earth and breathed into their nostrils the
breath of life, and they became living beings.

Living beings.

After a few years on this planet, really living seems a bit
idealistic. We are more likely to settle for making a living.
Most of us simply want the checkbook to balance at the end
of the month and the car to survive until the next Christmas
bonus. Life on this side of Eden is not what we hoped for. It
is not what we were made for. Something is missing.

So, we escape to a good story.

We enjoy a well-crafted plot. We like the drama of the
blockbuster movies and the *New York Times Best Seller
List*. If we're honest, we are searching for Eden in our fai-
rytales; we are searching for life. We think we are watching

our movies to escape from reality. But what if, within these stories, there exists some profound truth? What if we are escaping *to* some kind of reality?

It is no mistake that the human heart longs for story. We are living in one. Not the many accounts of how we fell in love or how the youngest recently got a raisin stuck in his nose. We have a million little tales that make up our life stories. But we are aware of something even bigger than our individual lives. We are living in what John Eldredge calls an epic Story that defines our reality. This reality is Truth, something that we post-moderns don't believe in. Truth, we believe, is subjective and cannot, therefore, be universal. But Truth does not depend on our perspectives. No matter how much we deny Truth, it doesn't go away. It is not altered by moods or seasons or weather. While we can lose sight of Truth, we cannot escape it, though sometimes we try.

The truth often hurts. To live wide open in a world that exploits our vulnerabilities is too painful, so we numb ourselves with the daily reality in which we exist. We try to stop feeling the depth of life, and we hide behind endless ways to cope. The day-to-day lacks adventure and becomes busy but just plain boring. We need more. We turn to movies and books because they offer us the adventure and meaning that no longer exists in the safe daily routine. But we need so much more than safety.

## THE NEED FOR THE SACRED

All children suffer from literal disease. If you have children, you know this. For example: If you tell a child not to punch someone, he won't. He will slap, smack, pinch, poke, and bite someone, but he won't punch. There was no fist, so it doesn't count as a punch. If you tell your daughter to pick up her clothes off the floor, don't be surprised if they are piled on her bed or in her closet instead. You didn't say to put them away; you said to pick them up off the floor. They are no longer on the floor. That's what counts.

If we are honest, a child exists in each adult as well. Just like children, we use literal facts to lawyer our way out of trouble. As long as we focus on the immediate, concrete reality in front of us, the specific words that someone spoke in the argument, the right angle to prove our point, we can survive on facts and completely miss the truth. We use facts to justify our decisions, to divert the focus from ourselves, and often, to confuse the truth. As Madeline L'Engle so aptly points out, "Literalism is a terrible crippler, but it does get us off the hook. Or do I mean the cross?"

A life full of facts is not necessarily a life of truth. Facts are cold, hard, and inanimate. Truth is meaningful, powerful, and alive. The *fact* is that Adam and Eve ate from the wrong tree in the Garden of Eden. The *truth* is that every level of our lives is impacted as a result. The *fact* is that Jesus was a real person in history. The *truth* ...well, He *is* the Truth.

We don't want to miss the Truth because we are only focused on the facts. We don't want to miss what God is offering while we argue and justify our version of the abundant life. We can master facts. We cannot master the Truth. Jesus not only spoke the truth, He is the Truth, and that is something that our finite brains have trouble grasping.

This split between fact and truth is the division between secular and sacred, knowing good and knowing God, and it rents the human heart in two. The sacred, we believe, is for church on Sunday and maybe Wednesday nights. Our secular lives are all the other parts: work, school, driving to the bank, sleeping in on Saturday, paying taxes. Rarely do the two intersect. But our secular stories are dry and meaningless. Mostly they are just busy. Our tangible, immediate, day-to-day lives bleed out the energy required to pursue our transcendent dreams and desires. We want more. Somewhere we know we were made for a glorious adventure, and yet it is the mortgage payment and the laundry that demand our attention.

All stories communicate some kind of truth. We get caught up in the epic dramas that reflect our true Story, the Story within which your life and mine is engulfed. A good plot is full of twists and turns, letting us know there is more going on than what the characters can see. Observing from outside the book or film, we know the storyline will eventually come to some kind of resolution. Living from inside our own stories, we have no idea where the plot is taking us. But we can know who is taking us there, and He has given us some clues as to how. The life Jesus promised transcends the secular, making our hectic stories sacred. When our individual lives become characters in the larger Story that God Himself is telling, something sacred happens. In God's Story, everything has meaning.

## GOD IS A STORYTELLER

When I take a picture of a sunset, I call it art. But my art is only an attempt to capture what the true Artist has already painted. When I write a story, I type words on a computer screen to stir the imagination within the reader. While I attempt to write words about life, God uses words to create it. My medium is paper. God's medium is life itself. He is telling His Story throughout Creation and in every individual He creates. Some reject Him. Some receive Him openly. The point is not how many reject and how many receive. The point to God's Story is how His character and His nature are displayed no matter how His creation treats Him: He is always faithful, always just, and always merciful. Always.

God used words and spoke the world into existence. His words became oceans and land and plants and animals and people. The first Epistle of John tells us that the Word became flesh and dwelt among us. Jesus is the Word of God, the same Word that spoke Creation into existence, so that all things were created by Him and through Him. My words say something. God's Word IS something, more tangible than the chair I'm sitting on or the pages you are reading.

What does this mean for me, a created being? God, the Storyteller, is trying to tell me who He is and who I am. If I can catch the moral of His Story, I can understand my role. I can understand why I'm here. My day-to-day life can have some sense of purpose, a sense of abundance. But I must be willing to surrender my storyline to something bigger. If I want an abundant life, I must be willing to lose the life I have now. This is not easy.

One of the greatest roadblocks to the abundant life is *my* perception of my own story. I have my drama. I have written my script. And in my production, I have given God the role of "Lord." I have given Him His lines (my version of prayer), and I have spelled out, in detail, exactly how He should emphasize each word. I know precisely how the story should progress if the "Lord" does His part, and I become very excited about *my* happy ending.

One problem: God is a terrible actor. He never reads His lines on cue, and He even changes them regularly. I can't seem to convince Him that He is messing up the whole storyline when He won't comply with my wishes. I wonder how He could really love me if He won't play along. After all, I did give Him the most important role in *my* story. He could at least follow the lines.

As we play this out, our disconnected experience of God convinces us that destiny is within our own grasp if we just try hard enough and play the scene to perfection. We believe that enough Bible study, prayer, and church attendance are the essence of the Christian life. If we put the formula together well (our version of obedience), we will reach our goals because God will then play out the lines we have given Him, leading to our happiness and success (our version of joy and peace), right?

The *fact* is that God created you and me. The *truth* is that God created us to be part of His Story. He is the point. He is the hero. He writes the lines and tells us what to do. Our Bible study, prayer, and church attendance allow us to become caught up in God's Story, not direct our own version of the "Christian life."

God is not only the Author of this Story; He is also the star. As egocentric creatures, we tend to think the Story revolves around us. In a way it does. Our lives are the stage on which God is performing His greatest masterpiece. All of God's goodness, mercy, grace, and redemption are displayed in our lives. But the point is God's goodness, mercy, grace, and redemption – not our lives. It is a subtle but important shift.

So if God is the point, we must begin with Him. What is His role in this cosmic epic? How do we recognize His part in all this? If we don't see clearly the role He has designated for Himself alone, we may try to take it on for ourselves. This always ends in disaster. We make terrible gods.

GOD'S ROLE

With reckless zeal, God identifies His role in the Story again and again. With each version of His name, He is declaring something about His character that informs us as to the direction the plot is taking.

He claims He is the Creator, Preserver, Master, and Lord. He is the Almighty, All Sufficient King. He is a Covenant God who heals, provides, sanctifies, sees our deepest parts, and delivers us. He is our Banner, our Peace, our Righteousness, our Judge, our Rock, and our Hope. He is the Shepherd, the Savior, the Redeemer, and the Most High God. He is the Lord of Hosts, the Mighty One, our Shield and Strength. He is Jealous, Holy, and Everlasting. He is Always There, First and Last, the Living God. He is our Father. He is our Husband. He is the Breath of Life. He Is.

This list is not exhaustive. The Bible gives us name after name describing God's character and role in this epic Story. Each name offers us more insight into God's nature and ability. In the prayer that Jesus taught His disciples to pray, He started with an honoring of God's name. We must begin with the holiness of God's name if we are to align ourselves with His Story. No wonder the Third Commandment tells us not to take His name in vain. Dishonoring His name dilutes the Story. We lose the impact of His role. Without that True North for our compass, we get lost in the secular mundane of the day-to-day. Wanting more, we try to take on His names for ourselves, attempting to be all-powerful, all-knowing, and the source of our own lives.

But our names are much different from His. We are called children, sheep, created beings, and dust, to name a few. In the context of Eden, these names were good. These names fit us well. Outside of Eden, these names make us vulnerable to the harsh reality of the fall. Children in our world are vulnerable and easily wounded. Sheep are made into sweaters and lamb chops. And we have hundreds of products on the market to bust dust. We resist the truth of our names. We feel defenseless. After the fall, names like orphan, widow, stranger, and lost became ours to endure. Ultimately, we bore the name enemy of God. Mankind ended up on the wrong side of the Story. We desperately need God's Name to be true. We need everything that He says about Himself to hold water, and hold us. And we need new names.

## OUR ROLE IN HIS STORY

We *are* children, but children of a King. We *are* sheep, loved so much that if we wandered off our Shepherd would leave ninety-nine other sheep to find us. We *are* created from the dust, but we bear the image of the One who created us. Our true roles in this Story were never meant to bring us shame, but to bring God glory. Without the connection to the Source of life, however, our individual stories are full of shame and despair. Without God our Hero, we are the damsel in distress who is never rescued. Without God our Healer, we are wounded beyond repair and without hope. Without Jesus our Shepherd, we are lost sheep, vulnerable to the attack of violent wolves. Without the breath of life, we are simply dust.

What fragile creatures we are. We truly are a mystery. How is it that we don't implode or simply blow away likes ashes? Some people can endure twenty bullets and live. Others are killed by random sticks. It is only by the breath of life that we rise above the dust, and once that breath is gone, we return to it. We are miracles. Can we experience this life to its fullest, if for no other reason than to honor the breath that gave it? How do we move beyond being counted as another casualty of death, wounded beyond abundance and fulfillment? This is the stage we've been given. The dramas that play out reflect how broken and lost we are. We need redemption, or most of our little stories are just sad. As Christians, we know the end of our Story, regardless of the storyline, will end in the arms of Jesus. But what about now? How does His Story intersect with ours?

Jesus said that He came to offer us abundant life, but this life is a paradox. Jesus died to offer it so that by His death we might live. In order to encounter such life, we must be willing, in a sense, to die as well: die to the masks we hide behind, die to the multitude of ways we protect ourselves. We must be more honest than ever before. In fact, the more open we are, the deeper the healing, the deeper the life. We must be willing to subject ourselves to God's Story of redemption. It is time to surrender to the theme of God's Story instead of trying to simply promote our own. God is still writing. God is still restoring. God is still God, and He's making all things new.

## MAKING ALL THINGS NEW

The theme of God's Story is woven into every individual life that offers itself to Him for redemption. God is healing, saving, guiding, completing, defending, and protecting right now. Our weakness is the stage for His strength. Our brokenness is the stage for His healing. Our experience of shame fuels His determination to save us. We are vital characters in God's Story about making all things new. He starts with you and me. He is writing our lives, inviting us to co-author our role and discover our names. What if hope is real? What if God can breathe life into our nostrils and give us abundance? What if His Story is true?

It's time to breathe again. It's time to take God at His word and claim the abundant life He has promised. It's time to discover our names.

Are you ready? Let the quest begin …

### Going Deeper

1. God is the author of all that we see. What kind of impact does that knowledge have on your everyday life? Does it impact you at all? If yes, in what ways?
2. Have you ever felt like there was a lack of meaning in your life? Describe your struggle.
3. Often we try to invite God into our stories to "fix" them rather than submit our stories to God's Story for redemption. Have you ever encountered this yourself? How did you work through it?
4. What names of God were you drawn to? Who do you need God to be for you right now?
5. What name for yourself do you most identify with right now? Why?
6. Does the name you have chosen bring you shame or comfort?

7. God is making all things new. Not some things, but all things. Where would you like Him to start in your life?

# 2
# The Lies that Bind:
## *Naming the Ways We Cope*

*"A story begins when our desires collide head-on with reality." Dan Allender*

*"Those who walk in great darkness have adjusted their eyes." John Eldredge*

*"The freedom question is not whether we can do whatever we want but whether we can do what we most deeply want." Gerald May*

*"No one ever has it 'all together.' That's like trying to eat 'once and for all.'" Marilyn Grey*

We have been invited into God's Story instead of reducing God to fit into ours. But doesn't it often feel like our stories are so powerful, so loud, it is difficult to persevere in that transcendent perspective? Sometimes an IRS letter feels bigger than the years of sermons teaching us to trust God in all things. A negative diagnosis spins us back to our most primal fears. And what to do about a horrible past? How do we reconcile the childhood stuff into God's Story? Was God even there?

It is time to travel back in our Story to grasp the impact of what happened "in the beginning." If we do not understand how deep the fall of mankind goes, we will not understand how good God really is; we will not understand how completely His grace covers us; we will not fully experience the salvation Jesus purchased for us. In short, we will miss the abundant life. Sometimes we need to see how much we have been saved from in order to experience the radical difference between a "before and after" life with God.

Let us start at our beginning. The world began. The stage was set: the sun shone, the oceans roared, the garden satisfied. God thought of everything. He made Eden for Adam and Eve and offered them freedom and dominion on the Earth. In the middle of the garden God placed two trees. The fruit of one tree was life. The fruit of the other was knowledge. The entire garden was built around this choice: which tree would be the source for Mankind?

We picked the wrong tree.

God declared the fruit of the tree of the knowledge of good and evil would be the death of us. Why not the tree of rebellion? Or the tree of bad choices? Or even the tree of sin? For some reason, God knew that the taking of the fruit of this particular tree as our source would be fatal to us. But why?

God knows good and evil. The knowledge of good and evil is an attribute of our Creator. The tree of rebellion or sin did not exist because these qualities do not exist with God. When Adam and Eve ate the fruit, they acquired an attribute of God but missed *Him* in their rebellion. In their disobedience, their relationship with God was ripped apart. What was left was knowledge without life.

We cannot manage an attribute of God without His presence, His life with us. Like a three-year-old trying to fly a giant cargo plane, God's attributes are so far above and beyond us that, when left on our own to direct them, we will surely crash. We cannot handle His strength or His wisdom or His knowledge without His 'oneness' with us. We don't get part of Him; we get the whole package. Adam and Eve forsook their relationship with God to attain His knowledge. Perhaps that is why Psalms, Proverbs, and Job repeat that it is the fear of the Lord that is the beginning of knowledge and wisdom. It is within our humble obedience and connection to God that we receive true wisdom and knowledge.

Adam and Eve traded knowing God for the knowledge of good. Forsaking their roles and wanting to take over God's role, they forgot their names. Instead of loving God, they wanted to *be* God. The guilt of their sin stripped them of their innocence and introduced to the human race the deep experience of shame. Left only with the knowledge of good and evil, but without God as our Source, we have been coping with the loss of our innocence ever since. A slow and painful ruin, this fruit of the knowledge of good and evil acts like kryptonite to Superman, sapping our very nature from us. Adam and Eve thought it would make them more powerful. In reality, it stripped them of their rule on Earth. The glorious crown of God's creation, made from the dust, was stripped of the breath that gave life and cursed to return to the dust. Cut off from God, they were left to depend on their own strategies for survival.

Hence, when the Bible talks of living from our 'flesh,' it is referring to this condition of coping without the Spirit of God to bring fullness. The apostle Paul describes his intense struggle with his own flesh when he writes: *"For the good that I want, I do not do, but I practice the very evil that I do not want"* (Romans 7:19). He describes a kind of bondage that prevents him from acting on his truest desires. He is clear that the struggle is, at times, overwhelming. In a way, Paul gives us the same permission to struggle with our own "stuck-ness." If God is no longer our Source for life, our flesh is all we have. We are truly in bondage to our sin.

Made to long, yearn, and need, our dependence on God gives our lives structure and purpose. Cut off from our Maker, we are left with the same yearnings and needs but without the One who can meet them. So why would God let this happen?

Love requires freedom. Without a sense of separateness, there can be no true oneness. God gave us the ability to be separate from Him so that we could fully and freely choose to be one with Him. The very ability to choose was intended to connect us but instead, because of free choices by Adam and Eve, drove us farther apart. The very parts of Adam and Eve that made them autonomous from God (their own bodies, their own perspectives, and their own choices for connection) became the incredible weights they had to carry to survive. As their children, we were meant to offer these autonomous parts of ourselves in submission to our Creator, not use them for our own purposes. But instead, our God-given desires and needs became cursed burdens that left us lusting for more without the ability to be fulfilled. When these "lusts" are not satisfied, we cope in very unhealthy ways. The survival strategies we use are actually sins.

Cut off from God, we are now what the Bible calls "of the world." Apart from God, the world offers little for us. But we are creatures who experience big things. As a result, our pure desires for connection are perverted into lusts. Our legitimate needs can only be met in illegitimate ways. Without God, our entire design is thwarted.

The apostle John, in his first Epistle, writes, *"For all that is in the world, the lust of the flesh and the lust of the eyes and the boastful pride of life, is not from the Father, but is from the world"* (2:16). Our disconnected souls must cope with the demands of these lusts and the results are even more disconnecting. The "lust of the flesh," when ignored, will lead to isolation and addictions. When the "lust of the eyes" is unsatisfied, we will experience the drive for entitlement or,

34

in fear, lean toward passivity. And when we fall prey to the "boastful pride of life," we forget how to surrender our lives to God's Story as we try to star in our own. Sometimes our coping is obvious, sometimes subtle. But trying to survive the fall is far different than living the abundant life. We need to name the obstacles that try to block us from God's best for us. Our challenge is to allow our private, often-secret strategies to surface so they can be addressed. Are you willing to open your heart and your mind and explore the ways you cope? I guarantee you will find yourself in at least one of the following places.

ISOLATION

Hypothermia is a condition brought on when the body temperature drops to less than 90 degrees Fahrenheit. When the body temperature drops below that, the body begins to shut down and the effects can be life threatening.

Isolation is emotional and spiritual hypothermia. Apart from others, our spiritual temperature cannot stay regulated. Our *ability* to connect begins to shut down and the *need* to connect begins to feel numb. Isolation keeps us insulated from the very connection that will bring us the abundant life. Our experience is one of survival as we face the tedious day-to-day facts but disconnect from the truth of our situation because we can't digest it. We develop ways to cope, or what psychologists call defense mechanisms. These coping strategies keep us from experiencing the often-unpleasant feelings of loss, pain, disappointment, betrayal, failure, and hopelessness.

The problem with isolation is that it's too cold to survive by ourselves. We were created to be part of a body. Spiritual hypothermia sets in and moves straight for the heart. Without connection to others, we will feel emotionally and spiritually frozen. Our experience is one of "numbing out" or feeling flat.

Just after I finished college and had my own apartment, I decided to cook something in the oven. I put my casserole dish on the top shelf and began to slide it to the center of the rack. As I pushed it, my hand touched the top of the oven. I heard a loud *psssst* and knew I was in trouble. My hand snapped back, dropping the dish. A nice raw line formed on the back of my hand where the skin had been seared off. I felt nothing … until about 45 minutes later when my purple hand felt like it was on fire. I asked the doctor (yes, I went to the doctor) why I didn't feel the burn at first. He told me that when there is a lot of pain in one place, the body sends so many signals to the brain that the brain shuts off all feeling for a while so that it can sort through the messages. Eventually, he said, the brain will send the pain that equals the injury.

The pain that equals the injury.

That is the experience of isolation. It is a sense of numbness that we live in so we don't feel the pain that equals the injury. But isolation gives us a false sense of control over our circumstances. In isolation, we develop hypothermia in the cold, cruel world. We were not made for isolation, but for connection and community.

The abundant life requires authenticity and the ability to be fully present with God and others. This means being fully present in our joys and in our pain. Isolation is one of the ways we cope with the relational hurts in our lives. But the ultimate relationship, the one we were made for, our intimate relationship with God, requires that we stop coping if we want to truly experience His fullness. We do not need to protect ourselves from the Healer. In fact, our isolation will keep us from the very Source we need to fully address the stuff we dread inside.

Ask the Holy Spirit to show you the areas in your life where you have isolated yourself, especially from Him. The purpose of this is not to "fix" what we do, but to simply become honest about the struggle. Listed below are a few ideas of how we do this:

1. Dissociation – a sense of "numb" in which we don't feel the intensity of the feelings associated with an event. This happens when we have not truly addressed the feelings, and we stay numb instead of working through them. Our feelings have split from the memories of what happened. We tell what should be a very emotionally charged story as if it is just information, like it happened to someone else a long time ago. Numb feels flat and depressing. Nothing seems fun. Relating to people feels exhausting.

2. Minimizing – when we say things like, "Other people had it much worse than me!" or "He only did it when he was drunk," or "The past is the past, and we have to get over it!" We minimize because the truth is so big that we can't digest it all at once. By making an event or circumstance smaller than it was, we think we will be able to swallow it easier. This is never true.

3. Shame – the belief that there is something uniquely wrong with me, and if I could just nail down what it is, I could fix it and make my life work the way other people's lives seem to be working. Shame is the experience of being judged and found wanting. As a result, we don't connect with other people, believing that if they really knew us they would not really like us. Shame keeps us away from what has hurt us in the past by not allowing anyone close enough to recognize what is lacking in us.

When we are isolated, our stories reflect these themes of dissociation, minimizing, and shame. We are lonely, overwhelmed, and emotionally exhausted. Isolation is light-years away from abiding, which is required to experience the abundant life. Isolation keeps us from what we most deeply need.

## ADDICTIONS

In order to really understand the impact of addictions on our lives, we need to first look at the freedom we have been given. In a sense, God has given us sovereign reign over our own lives. He designed us with the freedom to choose Him, and therefore, does not force us in that choice. *"It was for freedom that Christ set us free"* (Galatians 5:1). Christ's work of death and resurrection gave us back the freedom we lost in Eden. We are not robots or trained animals that simply follow orders and obey. When we freely choose Him, we find our deepest longings met and our most profound needs satisfied.

When we, instead, choose to remain as our own source for our wants and needs, we elevate those desires or needs to an improper place and develop shortcuts to satisfy them. That is a big statement. Let me say it again in another way: if God is not the Source for meeting our wants and needs, our only option is ourselves (sound familiar?). This means that we have promoted our own needs above God's presence in our lives. What was meant to connect us to our Creator (our wants and needs) instead drives us from Him as we fall into temptation and drift even further from our Source.

Temptation is all about shortcutting. When a relationship with Jack feels like too much work or becomes too painful, then Jack Daniels is waiting to satisfy. Are addictions that simple? Yes. When our hypothermic relationships leave us with emotional frostbite, we exchange them for behaviors we think we can control. Alcoholics Anonymous works because people who struggle with these addictions can say yes to others in the context of relationships so they are able to say no to the substance and behavior.

We are free. As a result, we choose what we will serve. The abundant life is experienced when we offer our freedom to God's service ... freely. Addictions bind us. Addictions force us to ask their permission to serve anything else. When we freely choose a self-serving behavior instead of God, addictions will steal our freedom. So what are we addicted to? Below is a list of traps that commonly bind us. Spend a few minutes, and ask the Holy Spirit to show you areas of your own life where you might be addicted.

1. Control – of ourselves, our stuff, our children, our spouses, our jobs, our money. We control to try to manage our anxiety when things feel chaotic. We are coping with an uncomfortable feeling in the flesh.

2. Substances – alcohol, drugs, prescriptive medications, nicotine, diet pills, food, anything that makes our bodies and minds feel better for a short time. We seek pleasure instead of appropriately addressing the desire.

3. Secret sin – anything we do that only we know about that takes the "edge off" how we feel about something. These secret "habits" are often sexual or even criminal (like stealing). Cutting has become a favorite secret addiction with teens and young adults.

4. Spending Money – to look good, feel good, to gamble, to escape the present situation.

5. Gossip – talking about other people to avoid dealing with our own feelings and to feel superior.

6. Sex and/or Pornography – physical union often becomes the most important part of connection with others, to the point of obsession and even control. And yes, sometimes women get addicted to sex and pornography, too.

7. Co-dependent Relationships – unhealthy friends seem better than no friends at all. When we want to

get healthier, these friendships pull us away from what will heal us.

Addictions are attachments that keep us from the freedom that Jesus purchased for us. They are what we use to cope with being fallen and having unfulfilled desires. When left alone, our addictions become our idols that demand our loyalty.

Addictions are the shortcuts we take to satisfy the flesh quickly. Over time, these shortcuts become the normal path we take to escape whatever doesn't feel good. At that point, we are no longer in control of them. They begin to direct how we approach the difficulties in our lives.

When Jesus was tempted in the wilderness, He had not eaten in forty days. Satan decided to appeal to Jesus' hunger. Jesus felt hungry (shocking), and Satan tempted Him to appease that feeling quickly by turning the rocks near Him into bread. Jesus stated that His food was every word that comes from God's mouth. God told Jesus to go to the wilderness and fast. He did not tell Jesus to make bread from stones. Even though Jesus was able, He chose obedience over independence.

Satan was tempting Jesus to operate outside of obedience: "*Satisfy that desire by using your power outside of obedience to God.*" In essence, Satan was tempting Jesus to forsake God's Story to begin to write His own. Jesus was not opposed to eating. Jesus was opposed to shortcutting obedience to satisfy His flesh. He had the freedom to choose to satisfy Himself, but instead chose to use His freedom in obedience to the Father. He knew that to satisfy His own flesh was to opt to forsake His dependence on God. Addictions are the result of habitually opting to satisfy our "lusts of the flesh" without God as the Source. We are all addicted to something. We are all attached to behaviors that keep us surviving but prevent us from really living. Ask God to gently point out your addicted attachments.

## ENTITLEMENT

I recently traveled to Rwanda, Africa, on a short-term mission trip. I was leading a counseling conference to train some pastors and lay-counselors in the recovery process as they continue to address the aftermath of the genocide that happened there in 1994. When we came to the idea of "entitlement" and the problems that this attitude brings about, my interpreter began to translate an entire paragraph for every sentence I spoke. While everyone seemed to understand the concepts very well, I realized that they did not have a word for "entitlement" that directly translates into their language. How can they address something as a problem if there are no words for it? How can we?

While the English language has this word, we do not necessarily know what it means. But entitlement is a very dangerous, very contagious, disease-like attitude that kills the soul and destroys our ability to relate to others and to God. We cannot afford to ignore it or treat it lightly. Entitlement steals the abundant life out from under us. This attitude leads us to believe that we are victims, stuck in a quality of life that is below what we really deserve. At its heart, entitlement is all about greed, a lust for more of what we see. In short, it is the lust of the eyes.

Adam and Eve did not believe in God's goodness. Instead, they believed that somehow He was holding out on them, denying them the knowledge of good and evil that they deserved. Entitlement killed them in the Garden of Eden, and it continues to kill us today. The drive for "fairness" screams from within our entitled hearts along with a demand for the scales to be tipped in our favor. But what if "fair" is not the point? Truly, what if we received what was fair? Given all the ways we cope with being fallen in this fallen world with other fallen people directing the same fallen stuff at us, do we want what is fair? If God were fair, we would all be in trouble.

And yet, how many of us demand more? We say things like, "I'm not changing until she does!" or, "Why should I respect him if he's not loving me well?" As we feed these lusts within us, we are killing our ability to relate. We *cannot* have relationship when we choose entitlement. It is the most dangerous attitude in the human dynamic. It began with God's enemy, Satan himself. Satan believed he should have more than what was given him. As his greedy lust for more increased, war in heaven broke out. Because he exalted himself, Satan was cast down and doomed by his own attitude. Convincing Eve, and Adam by default, that he was right, Satan led our first parents to their deaths. Entitlement kills the human heart. It is dangerous and must be avoided at all costs.

By the end of the day at our Rwanda Conference, our interpreter came up with a phrase instead of a word. He called entitlement "victim mind." I thought it stated the point very well. We must resist the temptation to fall into the lust of the eyes that demand we should have all we see. We must not allow entitlement to take root in our hearts as we seek to embrace the freedom and grace that God so richly pours out on us who believe. We need God's Story to be the transcendent purpose in our lives. Without Him, our lives are a quest for more and more without any satisfaction. Like eating cotton candy for dinner, it just doesn't satisfy. In fact, it might make us sick.

So what does entitlement look like in your life? How does it express itself in your heart? What are the warning signs for you that tell you that entitlement is creeping into your attitude? We must watch this one closely. Entitlement is the pride that goes before a big fall.

## PASSIVITY

Have you ever been driving at night when, suddenly, you see the glowing eyes of a deer standing 15 yards in front of your car? Swerving, dodging, and maneuvering, your heart races as your compact car becomes an off-road vehicle. The deer's passivity, or choice to do nothing, might just get him killed. And it certainly is not fun for the rest of us either! We often choose this method of coping with our own fear. We choose to do nothing, and that choice can create more problems than doing the wrong thing.

I had a friend once who made just enough money to pay the bills, but with no wiggle room. While she was *able* to sit down and pay the bills, she *didn't* sit down to pay the bills. The fear that her money would be all gone again drove her to avoid actually engaging in the act of writing checks and sending them. Instead, she would pray to win the lottery, hoping for some kind of "miracle" to launch her out of her financial situation. As a result, she had to pay late fees and interest that began a debt spiral that took a long time to repair. Was God ignoring her?

I had another friend whose husband was rather loud and passionate when he became angry. While he was not violent to her, he did scare her when he became upset. He had no idea she was afraid. He couldn't figure out why she would get a blank stare on her face, and it only angered him more that she wasn't responding. It seemed they were never coming to a resolution. She thought her silence was a way of avoiding conflict. She prayed that God would change him. Her choice to do nothing actually made the gap between them larger. Had God abandoned their marriage? Why wasn't He changing her spouse?

We use expressions like "a deer in the headlights" and "an ostrich with its head in the sand" as a way to express what people often do when they are afraid. But this kind of passivity actually creates more danger than safety. The deer often gets run over, and the ostrich is still visible to its predator.

James, the New Testament writer, tells us that we must be doers of God's word, not simply hearers only. If we simply know with our minds what is healthy and right, but do nothing to act on it, we will miss the abundant life that Jesus keeps offering. While it is helpful to hear good sermons, read good books, and attend workshops that give us new skills, if we do not apply what we have learned we will miss the whole point. What good is it to be literate but never read? How does it benefit anyone to spend thousands of dollars on ski equipment but never go skiing? In the same way, we cannot grow by simply listening to what God has to say without actually applying it. When God says forgive, He is not just giving us a theoretical idea that we should think about. We must do it. When He says He has forgiven us, we must step into that forgiveness and receive it, rather than wallowing in our own failures. If God states that He is the only one that can bind and heal our broken hearts, He is not asking us to ponder the beauty of that statement. He wants us to allow Him to actually bind and heal our broken hearts.

Passivity is the place in which we get stuck when we do not act on what we know. Usually our motivation is fear. But we are making a choice. We are choosing to do nothing, and most often this leads to far more problems than doing the wrong thing. God can't steer a parked car. If we are afraid of going the wrong way, at least our direction can be changed when we are moving. If we remain in one place, we will never change destinations. Passivity creates an environment of status quo where souls atrophy and life is reactionary as we try to protect something we often don't even want.

## INDEPENDENCE

Our final coping strategy is independence. We were designed to be completely dependent on God. Most of us would nod at this statement, but then reality hits. We pray and pray about something, and God seems silent. We begin to perceive God as undependable, unpredictable. We would never openly admit this, but our experiences scream that we must do this life alone. What doesn't kill us makes us stronger, right? We live a "Christian" life but our hearts are dying of unfulfilled emptiness.

When we are struggling with independence, we are looking for God's attributes to be the means to our own end. When we are stuck in this place of independence, we are actually still dependent. Our needs do not change, just our ability to receive what we need changes. And so our lives begin to reflect the subtle course change. We begin to depend on our ability to manage our sin instead of relying on God's grace and power.

Our logic is sound: we wrestle with our own personal responsibility in the process. Surely we have some kind of role to play in our own transformation, right? We don't want to be lazy. We know we must participate in what God is doing. So what is wrong with mastery and independence? Aren't we supposed to overcome? Yes, but ...

God not only wants to be our end, He wants to be our means. We ask for strength and wisdom not for the purpose of accomplishing our independent goals, however noble they may be. We ask for His attributes in order for Him to show up in a situation. We don't get His attributes without getting Him. God always offers Himself to us. Our role in this Story is not "Great Steward of God's Attributes." Our name is Child. Children require the care, support, and intervention of a loving Father not simply the capacity to manage that Father's abilities.

Independence is a dead-end that takes many forms. We create formulas or try to bargain with God, striving for obedience so God will answer prayers in a favorable way. Often times we ask for strength, wisdom, or peace without asking for God's presence. We don't want Him as much as we want His stuff. Sometimes we try to hide behind a sense of competence. We want others to believe we have it all together. This worldly perspective is subtle, isn't it? We are taught, especially in the United States, that independence is the most important value we have. Our independence is our freedom. But independence from God is bondage to sin.

God's solution to this problem of independence is simple. Like a scuba diver needs his oxygen mask, we need God. We don't just need Him for salvation (which we most certainly do), but we need Him for every moment of life on this planet. Imagine a diver taking one large breath of air and declaring that he has had enough. Imagine trying to live the abundant life by depending on your conversion experience alone to address the hardships in your story. We need a constant flow of God's presence to get us through. We don't need just His attributes; we need *Him*! He is the air we breathe.

Jesus invites us to think about Him on this level: He is the beginning and the end, the author of life and faith, and the healer of the many ways we have coped with being fallen. When we look to our own resources to manage our lives we are declining His invitation. We are living in very competent, very 'put together' sin.

## WHERE AM I?

If you are like me, you can see yourself in almost all these areas at any given time or situation. Aren't we creative in how we try to survive our broken-heartedness? The purpose of reviewing these areas is not to discourage but to name. We must name the ways we are coping in order to appropriately address them. In those moments when our stories reflect isolation or addictions, we desperately need connection with others and with God. Our dependence is reflected in our deep need for relational connection. When we are stuck in entitlement or passivity, we must begin to take some ownership of our lives and situations. When independence is our location on the map, we must learn to surrender our stories to the Story that God is writing.

We will look at this very closely in the following chapters but for now, locate where you are. What area (isolation, addictions, entitlement, passivity, or independence) best describes the theme to your story? Or maybe the question should be: what area best describes your story today? Can you see how the "natural" ways we survive keep us from really living? When we veer off the path into one of these areas, we will miss the abundant life and experience something very different: shame, guilt, and fear.

## Going Deeper

1. In your own words, what does isolation feel like?
2. What tends to rule your life more: shame, dissociation, or minimizing?
3. When we hear the word "addiction," we think of alcohol or crack. But when we see this word in the context of attempting to satisfy the lust of the flesh, we find we all have some addictions. What are yours?
4. We discussed that addictions are an attempt to shortcut our lives around bad feelings. What kind of feelings are we trying to avoid?
5. Entitlement killed us in the Garden of Eden. How does entitlement keep you from what you most deeply want in your relationships?
6. Under what circumstances are you afraid to take action, where you choose to do nothing and things become worse? Is this a struggle for you?
7. We need God in the same way a scuba diver needs his oxygen mask. What are other metaphors that describe our true dependence on God?

**3**

# Brokenhearted and Captive:
## *Naming the Cure*

*"We are in the presence of a good story when the flaw that shatters shalom is also the doorway to redemption." Dan Allender*

*"Perseverance is our supreme effort of refusing to believe that our hero is going to be conquered. Our greatest fear is not that we will be damned, but that somehow Jesus Christ will be defeated." Oswald Chambers*

## THE GOSPEL CURE

I was exhausted driving home from my junior year of college. I had pulled several "all-nighters" to finish all the term papers and exams needed to complete the year. As I was driving down I-81, crossing the Tennessee/North Carolina border, I dozed off. Suddenly my car made a terrible noise. I ran over the grated pavement on the shoulder that was placed there for just such a time. I jolted awake, saving my life (literally), and pulled immediately into the North Carolina welcome station as I crossed the State line. I slept in safety for about an hour, finding enough rest to make it home.

Spiritually, we drive off the road often. We are lured off course by isolation, addictions, entitlement, passivity, and independence, and risk our abundant life. We become addicted to relationships or avoid them altogether instead of connecting. We believe we have 'earned' our entitlement, or we have chosen to wait passively for life to come to us instead of owning the abundance we have been called to claim. Or we strive to be model Christians rather than allowing God to live His life through us. We not only go off course, we also get stuck on the shoulder in the weeds and soft earth. We become trapped in our methods of coping with the fall. The grated pavement, designed to warn us that we are off track, is the experience of guilt and shame. When we encounter these feelings, we need to pay attention.

But our language does not help our situation. If we have been in the Church for any length of time, we know there is a certain language (I call it Christianese) we speak fluently. We throw around words like grace, sin, justification, and (for the really fluent) sanctification. The blood of the Lamb who was slain justifies us. We get it. And yet ... we still struggle with shame and fear. Old messages that haunt us when we try to connect with others in intimate ways still bog us down. The experience of shame and guilt often permeates our everyday lives, even though we have been "justified by the blood of the Lamb." Our Sunday school answers don't fill the deep voids of the heart.

In the apostle Paul's day, the word 'gospel' was packed with meaning. The 'good news' was usually proclaimed within the context of winning a battle. When armies conquered their foes, messengers hurried to the small villages and towns to announce the 'gospel,' the good news of victory. The people had no idea they were free until the messenger of the gospel came to announce it to them. The citizens lived as though they were still in bondage, or in fear of attack by their enemies, until someone proclaimed their freedom had been secured.

Paul declares that we have been set free. We do not need to live as those who have driven their lives into the ditch and cannot get out. We must reclaim the meaning of this important word. If we don't, we will lose what our early Church Fathers grasped. We will lose the essence of what God has given us. And God has given us so much. He has given us the Gospel, and it is the cure for our guilt and shame.

GUILT

Guilt is designed by God to prick us when we have *done* something wrong. When we experience appropriate guilt, we feel a sense of conviction and move toward changing and/ or restoring our actions. Appropriate guilt is a God-given mechanism that keeps us on track. But there is another kind of guilt that is not so helpful.

Inappropriate guilt tells us that we have done something so wrong, or so many things wrong, that we are unredeemable. We fall into a trap. We say things like, "I know God has forgiven me, but I just can't forgive myself." In truth, we cannot forgive ourselves. This idea that we have the power to offend ourselves and then, somehow, forgive ourselves is independent thinking that ensnares the heart into bondage. If I offend myself, how am I to cancel the debt and pay it off myself? I am too close to the equation. We have never had the ability to forgive ourselves. Ever.

When King David was confronted by the prophet Nathan about his affair with Bathsheba and the murder of her husband, David penned some important words to God: "*Against you, you only, have I sinned and done what is evil in your sight*" (Psalm 51:4). So what about Bathsheba's husband? I think it's safe to say that if you murder someone you have sinned against the one murdered. So why would David say this?

King David understood something that we need to grasp. When we sin on any level, we have sinned first and foremost against God. We do not need to apply the process of forgiveness with ourselves. We need God to wash His forgiveness over us. We need to fully embrace the sacrifice of Jesus on our behalf in order to walk in the freedom He purchased for us.

Imagine you go to college and get your first credit card. Loving the fact that you don't seem to need real money, you run up $50,000 in debt. As you become aware that when you use a credit card you are, in fact, spending real money, you realize you are trapped by your foolish decisions. You cannot even make that much your first year out of college. Then, God writes you a check for $1,000,000. You take the check, crying in gratitude, fold it up, and place it in your pocket where it sits for years. Have you received His gift? Well, technically yes. But have you really *received* His gift or are you still trying to pay off the debt yourself? In the same way, if we do not apply God's forgiveness to our overwhelming debt of sin, we have not really received His forgiveness. We are stuck trying to forgive ourselves. Without God's forgiveness, the good news doesn't feel that good to us. Believe it or not, there is good news about sin.

The word 'sin' actually means 'to miss the mark.' When an archer aimed at his target and the arrow did not hit dead center, he was said to have 'sinned.' When we do not operate from a place of unity with God, we are sinning. We have missed the mark. This is why we cannot forgive ourselves. By not allowing God to forgive us, but instead feeling the need to independently forgive ourselves, we are sinning even more. Sin separates us from God. It always has.

God hates sin the way I hate car wrecks and gang violence. They kill people. Sin kills people. God loves people, so therefore He hates sin. To the same degree that God hates sin, God sacrificed to save us from it. God does not hate sinners. God hates sin. Big difference.

Sin is one of those words we don't use very much anymore. For many, it seems like an antique word used by people who spoke King James' English. The message of the Bible, they believe, is one of sin avoidance and sin management. Sure everyone sins, but as long as you don't sin worse than someone else, or you have a really good reason for doing it, then what's the big deal?

The problem is, we have lived in the dark for so long that our eyes have adjusted.

In God's Story, sin is such a big deal that He spent most of the Old Testament naming the different forms of it. He showed us how even Godly people like Moses and David sinned in ways that brought devastation to themselves and those around them. So how does God fix this?

Oswald Chambers penned one of the most profound declarations I have ever heard: *"God does not take responsibility for sin, but He takes responsibility for the possibility of sin and the proof that He does so is in the Cross of our Lord Jesus Christ."*

Think about that for a moment. What if God is not holding you and I responsible for what Adam and Eve did? What if He wants to rescue us from the nature we have inherited from them? What if this is true?

If Jesus bore our sins in His body, He has taken ownership of the consequences of sin. Stop. Reflect for a moment. Jesus has taken ownership of the consequences of your sin and my sin. When I look at guilt and shame, does this knowledge impact me at all? It means that God can work all things together for good for those who love Him and are called according to His purpose (Romans 8:28). Whatever I have done, or has been done to me, can be worked out ... for my good.

Does that mean that I may sin and not worry about suffering any consequences? No. I will experience the natural consequences of my choices. But God will use those consequences for my good. It means that anything I have done, or others have done to me, can be redeemed and will be used to chart the course for God's good in my life. In God's Story, everything comes back to God's goodness, even my sinfulness. He has justified me, and *that* is good news.

Uh-oh. There's another one of those Christianese words. We learn in Sunday school that justification means that God sees me "just-as-if-I'd never sinned." How is that even possible? I remember wondering if God had a terrible memory or if He just overlooks my sin. Both are far from the truth. We need to grasp the powerful impact of this word, and what it means for those of us who follow Jesus. To see this more clearly, let's examine His character.

By nature, God is both just and merciful. If we looked up those words in a spiritual dictionary, God would be the definition of both. He is completely just. He is completely merciful. He cannot cancel one to appease the other.

After the fall, these two character traits were no longer able to run parallel, but they suddenly intersected. In order to be just, God would have to punish Mankind. If He wanted to be merciful, He would have to turn His eye from what they did. So God did something radical.

Jesus became a human to take the punishment for Mankind. As Jesus' body was stretched out on that cross, His arms on one beam and His body on the other, at the very point of intersection, where mercy and justice meet, was His heart, both literally and figuratively. In order to maintain His perfect nature, God's heart had to break.

God was able to remain completely just and completely merciful at the same time. Who else could do that? Through Jesus, God met the righteous requirements of the Law, thus fulfilling justice. And because He bore it Himself, He was completely merciful. When He said, "It is finished," He was right. Our sinful souls have been purchased. Every thought, word, and deed we have ever had outside of our connected relationship with God has been procured. He has invited us to follow Him on this path of justification by calling us to trust in His nature.

Our journey leads us to this intersection, and we will encounter it on an almost daily basis. We must decide if we will depend on our righteousness, or if we will trust the work of Christ. Will we trust in our own ability to be righteous or will we count on the mercy of Jesus? Will we strive to forgive ourselves or will we cash the check?

Imagine that you build a boat to take you across the ocean. You name it the SS Titanic. One dark night you hit an iceberg, and pop a big hole in the side of your lovely ship. It begins to sink. As you try to figure out your survival plan, a lifeboat floats up beside you. On the side of that boat reads: SS JUSTIFIED. Someone else provided this boat for you. Are you willing to step off the boat you built? Are you willing to accept that you need someone else to save your life? Can you release the idea that you must create the boat that will bring you to safety? This is your intersection. Will you be justified by what you are able to do? Or are you justified by what Jesus has done *for* you?

If we choose the path of faith, that we are justified by nothing more than our faith, we jump into God's lifeboat and acknowledge that it is His boat that floats, not ours. God is asking for credit for what He has done to save us. When we can surrender this to Him from our hearts, then He credits this faith as righteousness. Our debt is cleared. We stand "just-as-if-I'd never sinned." That's amazing news!

## SHAME

While guilt tells us we have done something wrong, shame tells us there is something wrong with us. Shame is an experience, an undercurrent that drives many other feelings like fear and anxiety, and occasionally anger. Sometimes it is subtle, sometimes strong. But at its core shame is the experience of being judged and found wanting. More specifically shame says, "There is something uniquely defective about me, and if I could just figure it out my life would work the way other people's lives seem to be working." We feel we are being punished for something, and we may not even know specifically what we have done. Shame is what causes us to strive to be good enough, strong enough, smart enough, just enough.

While shame feels very personal, exclusive to me, it is universally encountered by every person who has ever walked the earth, save one: Jesus. Those who are out of touch with their shame – we call them shameless – have other serious issues, for we have all been judged and found wanting. None of us survived the fall. The fact that all people experience shame is evidence that God's word is true. All of us know that something is missing in us, and we are not as glorious and complete as we were designed to be. Something *is* missing.

Humanistic psychology offers a cure. They call it self-esteem. *If we could just learn the unique specialness within us and embrace it, we would no longer experience that sense of lacking.* This is what I call "Wizard of Oz theology." This view of God is limited to a personal experience or even preference. Those who ascribe to this view of God ask Him to make them great, or at least better. But then, as they pursue their greatness (so self-esteem teaches), they find that "God" is not really a powerful god at all because really what was lacking was in there all along.

As a culture, we tend to lean toward this view of solving our shame problem. We teach children to love themselves no matter how anyone else feels toward them, to believe in themselves even against their constant shortcomings, and to feel good about their efforts even if they fail. So how do we know when we have enough self-esteem? How much is too much? Are we producing entitled narcissists? Isn't this the same kind of independent, self-focused thinking that runs our car right off the road?

I have a Mickey Mouse doll that I received in the second grade. He is no longer black but a kind of deep blue. His ears are flat against his head; the wires inside that gave his ears shape crumpled up from years of sleeping under my arm. His eyes have fallen off several times and are now glued on, though a bit off center. They are colored in orange since we didn't have a peach colored marker. His felt shorts are barely intact. He looks nothing like a Mickey Mouse from Disney World. If I were to try to sell him in a garage sale, I wouldn't get ten cents for him.

But if my house were on fire I would grab him first. While Mickey is just material and stuffing in an unattractive package, he was my velveteen rabbit. You could not buy him from me for a million dollars. So how much is Mickey really worth?

You and I are dust and breath. We isolate, we become addicted, we are passive, we feel entitled, and we try to handle our lives independently. We fall short of our design. We are judged and found lacking. Shame tells us that our worth is directly connected to this deficit.

This is the lie.

Just as I determine Mickey's worth as his owner, God determines our worth as our Creator. Apparently, we are worth the price of His Son.

And so, once again, the Gospel becomes the cure, this time for our shame. Shame tells me that I suffer because of my ambiguous defect, and while I may be angry about it sometimes, I secretly believe that I probably deserve it. If I could figure out the formula for abundant living then I would deserve to thrive. If my life is hard then I must deserve it somehow. After all, I believe that my worth and my ability to live a righteous life are intertwined. Inseparable, I must strive to be "good enough" to avoid more judgment.

But what does the Bible really say about judgment?

The Bible talks about two different kinds of judgments. The Day of Judgment is the time in history to come when God will proclaim His sentence on Satan and those who do not follow His Son. The Bible refers to this time as the "day of judgment" or the "day of the Lord."

This judgment does not apply to those who follow Jesus.

The Bible also describes a judgment that happens when God allows us to experience the natural consequences of our choices. For example, if I run up my credit cards, no matter how much I pray, I will not win the lottery to pay them off. If I drive like a maniac believing that I have guardian angels to protect me from my consequences, I will find myself in a hospital or a jail and not understand how God could let this happen. God does not stop Christian teens from getting pregnant, or transform the chocolate cake to a zero calorie dessert because we said grace.

Instead, God allows the natural consequences of our choices to stand. He allows us to decide what we want. So what do you want? If you say you want to fit into your clothes from two years ago then stop trying to bless the calories out of the cake, and quit eating it. If you eat it, then just know you wanted the cake more than you wanted those expensive jeans back.

These natural consequences are based on the reality in which we live here on this planet. But these reality consequences are not relational consequences. In other words, God doesn't *feel* differently about us when we sin. Sure, He is grieved when we sin, but He doesn't hold grudges or dislike His children because we mess up. As Christians, the consequences of our choices are discipline. God is working through our choices to teach us to trust and depend on Him. Like rebellious children, we often mistake His correction for an attempt to control us. So here comes an intersection on our journey: we must choose the wide path or the narrow path. The wide path of shame leads us to poor choices, which leads to condemnation, which leads to more bad choices. Repeat, rinse. The narrow path of understanding God's judgment leads us to know, because of our salvation, that all our choices are used for our ultimate good, leading us to better choices. God will allow us to experience the natural consequences of our choices, but He will always use them to teach us a better way. It is our job to be good students. So how can His just nature allow Him to do this?

Jesus bore our shame for us. He took on God's judgment for you and me so we could pass through judgment into life. Let's look at Romans 8:3-4:

> *For what the Law could not do, weak as it was through the flesh, God did: sending his own Son in the likeness of sinful flesh and as an offering for sin, he condemned sin in the flesh, so that the requirement of the Law might be fulfilled in us, who do not walk according to the flesh but according to the Spirit.*

Sit with this for one moment. Let it sink in. What was defective about you has been fixed in Jesus. Jesus filled in what was found lacking in you. Shame, then, has no place in your heart or life. Jesus bore your shame and mine. Judgment is no longer an issue. As for the Day of Judgment ... we will pass right through. We no longer have to fear God's judgment in any form. *That* is good news. So how can God do this? How can He, a God of justice, allow me (a sinner) to pass through judgment when sometimes, even as a Christian, I still sin?

## ROOTS AND FRUIT

I have never witnessed a tree trying to create fruit. Imagine an orange tree, squeezing and grunting, trying to make an orange pop out of a branch. Imagine an apple tree with a constipated look trying to force an apple from one of its limbs. I just can't see it, can you? What would a constipated tree look like anyway? Trees don't strive to produce fruit. It just comes.

The type of seed planted determines the fruit of a tree. If I want to grow tomatoes in my backyard, I need to plant tomato seeds. If, by mistake, I plant green beans, it will not matter what my intentions were or how badly I wanted tomatoes. My heart could have deeply wanted tomatoes. Maybe I even told everyone how excited I was about my tomato plants. But if I planted green beans I will get green beans. Period.

If I say that I want to live the abundant life, but I plant the seed of entitlement or addiction, I will not grow the abundant life. No matter the 'good reasons' for my passivity or independence, or how I need an outlet, or how I can't help it, those seeds will not produce life. I must plant into my life what I want to sow in my life. Galatians 6:7-9 says it this way:

> *Do not be deceived, God is not mocked; for whatever a man sows, this he will also reap. For the one who sows to his own flesh will from the flesh reap corruption, but the one who sows to the Spirit will from the Spirit reap eternal life. Let us not lose heart in doing good, for in due time we will reap if we do not grow weary.*

If I want to reap the promises, blessings, and presence of God, I must sow into my heart the things that connect me to Him, that humble me before Him, and cultivate a life that reflects health and wholeness in Him. We will address this in detail beginning in the next chapter. But for now, we must understand this "law of the harvest" idea. What we plant will grow. Jesus stated this concept when He was talking about discerning false teachers from those who speak for God. In Matthew 7:16-20 He says:

*You will know them by their fruits. Grapes are not gathered from thorn bushes nor figs from thistles, are they? So every good tree bears good fruit, but the bad tree bears bad fruit. A good tree cannot produce bad fruit, nor can a bad tree produce good fruit. Every tree that does not bear good fruit is cut down and thrown into the fire. So then, you will know them by their fruits.*

All of us, since Adam and Eve, were born with a sin problem. We were all born disconnected from God. Therefore, at our roots, our source of how we survive is a sin nature. Look at the picture below:

What kind of tree are you?

Sin          Spirit

When *sin* (the noun, meaning the condition of) is at the root, the fruit are sins (the verb, meaning the actions). The *sin* that has disconnected us from God since Genesis 3 produces in us sins, actions that align with what has been planted in us. It is this condition of *sin* that causes shame. It is the actions of sins that cause feelings of guilt. So God has done something amazing. He has taken our *sin* upon Himself in Jesus and replaced our root source with His Spirit. This is so important for us to grasp. God, through Jesus, is offering His Spirit to us as a Source for our lives. He wants to replace our sinful methods of coping in our individual stories by rooting us in Him as the Source of life. He wants to make us new creations (see 2 Corinthians 5:17). By becoming our Source, the fruit of the Spirit can begin to manifest in our lives.

Just as a tree does not strive to produce fruit, we do not strive to love more, have more joy or peace, or work harder to be patient. The fruit comes from the root. If the root is *sin*, we will produce sins. If the root is the Holy Spirit, His fruit will grow in our lives. It's that simple.

So why do Christians still sin? The apostle Paul struggled with the same issue. As stated earlier, he did the things he didn't want to do, but then neglected to do the things he wanted to do. He felt trapped in his behaviors just like you and me. But Paul recognized something that we need to catch. He realized that when he was acting in such a way that he did not reflect God's Spirit as his Source, it was not him but *sin* (the noun) in him that did it (see Romans 7:19-20). He recognized that sometimes something outside of his character caused him to sin (the verb). This was not "the devil made me do it" kind of scenario. Paul was saying that even though the Spirit was his Source, sometimes a rotten piece of fruit came out. Paul experienced guilt (because of sins) but not condemnation or shame. He did not own the sinful nature that once ruled him. Instead, he embraced his freedom from *sin* by the Spirit of life.

When we confess our sins, God will not only forgive our sins but also cleanse us from all unrighteousness (1 John 1:9). As Christ-followers, rooted in God's Spirit, we will often still produce rotten fruit. We will still isolate. We will still fall into entitlement. We will still sin. But here's the promise: when we confess the fruit, God takes care of the root. He gives us new life from the root up.

This gives us a whole different perspective on the "Christian life." This is not about sin management. This is not about striving to be good enough. We do not try to control the fruit. The fruit tells us what we are depending on to be our source. Is it our sinful survival techniques (isolation, addictions, entitlement, passivity, and independence) or is it God's Spirit? We will know by the fruit produced in our lives.

## FRUIT OF GOD'S WORK

Once upon a time, God made people. He loved people with all of His heart. But people sided with His enemy and betrayed Him. They chose to disconnect from Him. This was unacceptable to the Creator who passionately loves His creation. God promised to defeat His enemy through Eve's seed (Jesus – see Genesis 3:15) and sowed Jesus into His Story from the beginning. We are His harvest.

Let us not forget we are living in His Story. Our inability to remember this important detail drives our lives off course, into ditches, and off cliffs. When we remain firmly rooted, by the Holy Spirit, in God's Story, we will see Him do things that only He can do. If we have been offered abundant life, why on earth would we want to settle for simple survival? Why experience inappropriate guilt, shame, and fear if these feelings are not needed to overcome sin? Why strive to produce good fruit when all that is needed is to rely on the Spirit as the root Source? His fruit will then come naturally.

We have discussed in detail what God has, can, and will do in our lives. We've looked at how we get off track and what God does to get us back. So what is our role? How do we participate? This is our starting place. We begin by joining God in His Story and naming where we are instead of trying to figure out how God fits into our little stories. Maybe you are "in the beginning" of your walk with God. Maybe you have been walking with God so long and know Him so well that you know how many hairs are on *His* head. But we begin with a relationship with Him. Within that context, we can explore where our lives jumped the tracks (isolation, addictions, entitlement, passivity, or independence) and name our guilt and shame. This is something we can do with the guidance of the Holy Spirit. Let Him help you find His gospel cure.

The second thing we can do is own what is ours. The next section is all about ownership and how it, when we become good at it, gives us the freedom to live the abundant life. We own where we are, how we think, what we say, and what we hold onto. Ownership is the key to the freedom.

The third thing we are able to do is surrender. We will look at this very closely in section three. Section four is all about living it out. So the rest of our journey is about our participation in the rescue mission of our hearts by God. In a sense, He allows us to join forces with Him as He sets out to free us from the enemy, with whom we once sided, to regain our child-like hearts that are so valuable to Him. We cannot save ourselves. We can, however, connect; we can own; and we can surrender.

## Going Deeper

1. How do you typically respond to God's discipline? Are you grateful? Do you feel judged?
2. What does it mean that God is not holding you responsible for what Adam and Eve did?
3. Receiving God's forgiveness is difficult. Have you received His check by putting it in your pocket, or have you cashed it? Don't answer quickly. Think about it.

4. Is trusting God with changing our hearts passive? Are we irresponsible if we don't strive to stop sinning?
5. What is our part in this process? What is God's?
6. Which tree do you most identify with? Why?
7. What does it mean if a Christian sins?

# Owning...

- To possess; hold as personal property, to have
- To admit; recognize; acknowledge; to confess

*"Until I have worked through self, I will not be enabled to get out of the way." Madeline L'Engle*

Relationships require the right tension between together and separate, oneness and autonomy. In marriage, for example, it takes two people to become one. Our relationship with God is the same. We must know ourselves to know Him and we must know Him to know ourselves. We are separate but one. Ownership is the essence of how we maintain the right tension.

# 4
# Created in His Image: *Owning Our Design*

*"Each member of the Trinity points faithfully and selflessly to the other in a gracious circle."*
Frederick Dale Bruner

*"God wills that we should push on into His presence and live our whole life there. This is to be known to us in conscious experience. It is more than a doctrine to be held; it is a life to be enjoyed every moment of every day." A.W. Tozer*

*"To find joy in another's joy is the secret of happiness." George Bernanos*

In the beginning, God created light and said it was good. He made land and plants and said it was good. Then He made the stars, the sun, and the moon and said it was good as well. God created the sea creatures and the land animals and said (you guessed it) that it was also good. Then He said, *"Let us make man in our image, according to our likeness"* *(Genesis 1:26).* So He made Adam, but Adam was alone. God declared this was not good. Adam was created in God's image, and God has never been alone.

In the Hebrew, the word for "God" in Genesis 1:26 is *Elohim*, a plural word. The verbs used, however, are singular, expressing that while this God is plural, He is also singular. It would translate something like "they is" or "several was." Now I live in South Georgia, and many here would not hear the problem with this grammar, but this is very intentional language used to convey a sense of community within the Godhead. God is a small group made up of Father, Son, and Holy Spirit, who live in constant submission and perfect unity.

## THE FELLOWSHIP OF THE TRINITY

Jesus was clear that everything He did was out of obedience to the Father. The Father clearly exalts the name of Jesus above every other name. The Holy Spirit never attempts to spotlight Himself but instead always shines on what God the Father and God the Son are doing. The relationship of oneness described in this is so intimate and integrated it is hard to comprehend. Each member of the Trinity has the power of the Godhead, and yet each member willingly submits that power to the other. It becomes a constant circle of total submission.

We were created in this image. We are powerful creatures who, within the context of that power, submit to others willingly. Bob Dylan was right when he said that we're "gonna have to serve somebody." Our design requires it. We have explored the ways we serve ourselves, appeasing the lusts of the flesh. We know this kind of service does not heal or even satisfy. It does not work because we were never meant to do it. Pointing to ourselves this way destroys us by destroying our relationships and we were not created to be alone.

No member of the Trinity ever points to Himself. Ever. In the same manner, God instructs husbands to point to their wives, wives to point to their husbands, children to point to their parents, parents to point to their children. He tells bosses to treat employees with respect and for employees to do their work as unto the Lord. He tells us to love our neighbors as we would love ourselves and to lay our lives down for our friends. God can ask us to do this because His is the image that inspired our design, and this is how He relates. We were made for it. It is what is most true about us. But it sure doesn't feel like it.

## CUT OFF FROM THE SOURCE

The 'fruit incident' in the Garden of Eden really messed things up. We must stop minimizing what happened there and deal appropriately with the consequences of that day. Marriages were never meant to be this hard. Parents were never meant to grieve the waywardness of their children. Friends were never meant to betray each other. Work was supposed to be fulfilling. Relationships were supposed to last forever. The breath of life was supposed to be our Source for every thought, emotion, desire, plan, and dream. We were made to be one with God and each other.

In the absence of the Source, we turn to each other, to ourselves, and to our work to satisfy those deep places. Without the breath of life, we settle for romance and lust as our solution for oneness. Women want romance. What do the romance novels, chick flicks, and soap operas offer? The knight in shining armor fights for her, loves her unconditionally, and points to her above anyone else.

Men are also looking for oneness, for intimacy, but without God as the Source it easily becomes lust. The pornography industry testifies to this. Pornography addiction is epidemic, even in the Church, even among those in ministry. A man, like a woman, wants to be wanted, for someone to point to him above anyone else.

We are groping around in the dark, trying to find connection and oneness that will fill the empty space where God once lived "in the beginning," when He breathed life into us and made us living beings. And so, Jesus comes into the scene to bring us the breath of life once again.

## GOD POINTS TO US

As a member of the Trinity, Jesus did something incredible: He gave up His place in heaven and became one of us. The second chapter of Philippians tells us that He did not consider equality with God something to be held onto, but gave it up to serve the Father. This was not out of character for Him. Jesus has been submitting to the Father since ... well, forever. This is how they have always related. Jesus always serves the Father. So what was the Father trying to accomplish by sending His Son? We find the answer in John 3:16: *"For God so loved the world that he gave his only begotten Son, that whoever believes in him shall not perish, but have eternal life."* God the Father wanted to give us back real, eternal life.

So what is this eternal life about? Heaven? Something else? Jesus answers that question for us. At the very end of His life on Earth, Jesus prayed for us, declaring to His Father, *"This is eternal life, that they may know you, the only true God, and Jesus Christ whom you have sent."* (John 17:3).

This word "know" is an important word. In the Greek, it means a deep, experiential knowledge. It implies such an intimate understanding that first century Jews used the word as an idiom for sexual intercourse. Think about this for a moment. Eternal life is deep oneness and intimacy with God. Jesus said He came to give us abundant life, abundant connection with the One who created us. Follow this closely, and it will change your life. The Father, desiring oneness with you and me, asks the Son, who willingly complies, to become one of us. Jesus points to the Father so the Father can point to us so we can point to Him. God is inviting us into His fellowship. The Father sent the Son. The Son sent the Holy Spirit. The Holy Spirit sends you and me. When we invite Jesus into our hearts, God invites us into His.

The Celtics drew a symbol for the Trinity that demonstrated this flow of relationship, perfect in unity. He is inviting your heart and mine into the center of Himself.

The Story we are living in is about this amazing love of God. So often, we approach our Christian lives as though it is all about how we love God. But He loved first.

Think of a tennis game. God served first by offering His Son. We can only play this game because He started playing with us. It was while we were yet sinners that Christ came and died for us. We refused to play with Him but He pointed to us anyway. God always points out. He is inviting us to point back. The sanctification process is how God teaches us to volley with Him.

Matthew 6:33 gives us a picture of this: *"But seek first His kingdom and His righteousness, and all these things will be added to you."* When we seek God as our Source, He takes care of everything else. Not some things. Everything. If you want God's strength, point to Him. If you need His wisdom, point to Him. If you need hope, joy, or self-control, point to Him. This is His Story remember? Loving us enough to protect us from ourselves, God does not offer His attributes for our own consumption or use. God is not a resource; He is the Source.

## THE NAME OF THE GAME: CONNECTION

*"He is before all things, and in Him all things hold together"* (Colossians 1:17). Just as a wheel finds it shape and strength in its design around the hub, everything that is real finds its being and definition around Jesus.

Our finite little brains tend to think linearly and in terms of efficient outcomes. Like learning the rules to a new game, we strategize about how to play well in this Christian life game. When we pray, we have thought through what is required for a specific outcome and we are asking God to be the supplier of whatever is missing for our outcome to work. So what's wrong with that? Shouldn't we pray for God to fill in the missing pieces? Doesn't He promise to answer when we ask? So why doesn't He every time? Sometimes it seems He has disappeared. How does this game work?

We often approach God for what He can do to help us efficiently accomplish what we need done. We want things to be "nailed down" and dealt with "once and for all." He can help us get the loan, or help a child to feel brave. This is true. He can do all these things.

Our independent hearts and minds, however, lead us to a place of striving. We strive to hold down the job, the family, and all the expectations of living here. We are trying to hold it all together. If we are really honest, we can admit that we view Jesus as one of many options we have to hold our worlds in order. We wonder why the Christian life is so hard and doesn't always seem to work so well. But what if we are playing the wrong game?

What if His blessings come through Him, not from Him?

What if we receive His life by being 'in Him' rather than near Him?

The way a light does not work until it is plugged in, our Christian lives don't 'work' until we are in Christ. A lamp, sitting next to an outlet, does not light up until it is connected to the source of power. The power of God to transform us does not work because we do what Jesus would do. We must enter a oneness relationship with Him, be in Him, to experience Him holding all things together in our lives. And so, when we are abiding in Christ, whatever we ask for will be answered in Him. Whatever the outcome, He is the answer.

When we try to access God outside the context of this oneness, we are trying to play a different game. Nothing will hold together. He first invited us into His game by serving His Son, lobbing the ball in our court. We accept this gift (our conversion), but then often walk off the court and wonder why our lives don't change. Our language reflects this idea: We say, "I have received Jesus as my Savior." This is true, but it's only the beginning. We say the prayer, we get baptized, and then we often stop. We get so caught up with our car payments and to-do lists that we don't realize we have missed the ball that God is offering back. We step onto a tennis court, hit the ball once, and call it a game.

When we choose to stay on the court, we will be changed. We will be asked to offer, sometimes in small pieces, every part of who we are and serve it over the net. As we offer ourselves, pointing to God, He offers Himself, pointing to us. We give Him what is ours. He gives us what is His. No longer do we consider what is ours as our own possession but rather something else to offer to Him. He, who did not even spare His own Son, is willing to offer us whatever we need. We begin to exchange what is in our hearts, good or bad, for all that is in His heart. We exhale ourselves and inhale Him in an amazing breathing-type motion that begins to change everything about us to the deepest levels. This is the art of breathing. We never leave our air supply.

A scuba diver would never claim to only need one big breath of air before diving. No one eats "once and for all." In the same way, we cannot live out our Christian lives based on one conversion experience or baptism event. We must learn the art of breathing out what is ours and breathing in what God is offering. We must stay on the court and keep playing this connection game. As we abide here, remaining in Christ, we change from the inside out. But we do not do this in isolation. God has given us many different kinds of relationships to show us how this looks.

## HUMAN REFLECTIONS OF CONNECTION

Throughout Scripture, God gives us instruction on how to relate in the same manner as the Trinity, a manner that aligns beautifully with our original design. These relationships help us to experience and practice the connection game that God invites us to play with Him. These relationships were never meant to replace our relationship with God, but to reflect and act out in concrete form the relationship we have with Him.

*Marriage.* Relationships do not get more intimate than marriage. One flesh. That's pretty close. As a result, we are asked to live in that "Trinity-like" relationship with a spouse.

She points to him by respecting him. He points to her by loving her as Christ loves the Church. Not only did Jesus die for the Church, He lives for her, too. The result of this mutual pointing is oneness.

The purpose of marriage is to point us to Christ. Having someone to grow old with is a perk, but it is not the purpose. Being compatible and having fun with someone is wonderful but not the purpose of marriage. God gave people the gift of marriage to teach them the level of oneness He wants to have with them. If you want to read more about this level of intimacy with God, read the Song of Solomon ... it's the PG-13 version of God's love for His people. He is using a language from marriage so that His people can understand how deeply He loves them and what He means when He talks about being a husband to us. Jesus speaks the same way to His Church. His ultimate desire is for oneness with His people.

Marriage is the living metaphor God uses to help us experientially understand how to be one with someone outside of ourselves. It is training for submission to God. While God is interested in happy marriages, He is more interested in holy people. Think you don't struggle with selfishness? Get married. Think you don't struggle with anger? Get married. Marriage is an important relationship that brings up all the junk inside that keeps us from pointing out. God does not require marriage to teach us these things but He does use it for many as a refining furnace. Iron sharpens iron. And sharpened iron can point out.

*Parenting.* The word *abba* in the New Testament is an Aramaic word for *father* that could be translated *daddy*. The word implies a tender familiarity, reflecting an intimate and caring relationship between a parent and a child. God has offered us the honor of using that name for Him. Romans 8:15 says, *"For you have not received a spirit of slavery leading to fear again, but you have received a spirit of adoption as sons by which we cry out, 'Abba! Father!'"*

God, our *Abba*, teaches us how to point to our children because He is pointing to us in the same way. God gives us children so we can see through His eyes the way He looks at us. Because we have all had parents, we understand what it is like to be someone's child, the concept that we are adopted into God's family, and that we are His heirs. The parenting relationship God offers is one way we can understand the extent of His love for us.

The Book of Proverbs has much to say to parents and equally as much to say to us as God's children. The following passages highlight God's heart towards us, His children.

- *"Discipline your children while you still have the chance; indulging them destroys them"* *(Proverb 19:18, The Message).*

- *"Point your kids in the right direction—when they're old they won't be lost." (Proverb 22:6, The Message).*

God knows that without discipline we will become corrupt. But who likes discipline? It is through this discipline however, in the context of a parental love relationship, that God transforms us.

God gives children to adults so we can continue to grow up. When the love is pouring out of our hearts for our children, we gain a small insight into the depth of God's love for us. At the same time, the selfish nature of children reminds us how we still need parenting as we see that same nature reflected within our own lives. Parenting is not an end in itself. Parenting teaches us to point out.

*Authority.* Few topics trigger a sense of rebellion faster than authority. If I say, with authority, that you should not think about dancing pandas, what goes through your mind? If I say you should obey the speed limit, what do you want to do? How many parents ask their children to clean their rooms only to debate who actually owns the room? We typically resist authority for fear we will lose our power. Nobody likes to be over-powered. And so, we often either obey out of fear of the consequences or we just rebel.

But power and authority is not the same thing. Authority is not supposed to make us feel powerless. Power is something we all have. Authority is something that only some have. In the Biblical sense, authority is never allowed to take power from someone. Authority is there to direct someone's power for the common good. We are to submit our power to the authority God has placed in our lives, whether that is a parent, a teacher, a boss, or a government official.

Power over one's own life is called self-control. Self-control goes beyond minimizing a temper-tantrum or frugally saving money. Self-control is how we own what is ours and choose what we do next. We can use our power for good or for evil and it is our decision as to how we will wield it. Submission is having power and *choosing* to surrender it to authority. Submission is not powerlessness. In the context of pointing out, power is our index finger, and authority is where we are asked to point it. We are able to use our power for anything. We are asked to submit our power to authority.

God has ordained several areas of our lives to practice this submission. At home, we practice submission as children who submit to parents through obedience, as wives who submit to husbands through respect, as husbands who submit to wives through protective love. In the workplace, we practice submission with the boss and those who sign our paychecks. In the community, we submit ourselves to the laws of the land, to the governing authorities.

If you are powerless, you cannot submit. If you feel powerless today, start there. Ask God for the freedom to become His bondservant. Galatians 5:13 states, *"It is absolutely clear that God has called you to a free life. Just make sure that you don't use this freedom as an excuse to do whatever you want to do and destroy your freedom. Rather, use your freedom to serve one another in love; that's how freedom grows"* (The Message). We are allowed to protect our freedom, not for the sake of entitlement and our "rights," but so that we have something to offer the authorities God has placed in our lives.

When we embrace this calling to submit to authority, we are opening ourselves to something profound. We do not become weaker; we grow stronger. When we stand fully in our own power and freely lay it down, we look like Jesus. We are able to give freely from the heart because we are not seeking more power through our actions.

Pointing to those in authority also trains us in the way of humility. We learn how to give up our own agendas to fulfill someone else's. Isn't this an important concept in our walk with God? Don't we need to be able to give up our stories for His Story? God has placed authority in our lives, not to make us powerless, but to teach us how to wield the amazing power He has placed within us. 1 Peter 2:16 says," *Exercise your freedom by serving God, not by breaking the rules" (The Message).* God has set us free, in Christ, so that we may freely love and serve Him. Submitting to authority works through those places within us that demand our own way and teaches us how to yield our power. It is this God-given power that enables us to point at all.

*Friends*. True friendship is a sacred thing. Unlike marriage, there are no legal bonds to keep it together. Unlike parenting, there is no obligation to protect and nurture the other. Friends do not hold a one-up position of authority in our lives either. The only force holding friendship together is the desire to be there. There are no "have-to's" or "should's," just "want-to's."

Jesus is our friend. He is a friend who sticks closer than a blood relative. While He takes on the responsibility for saving and healing us, His core motivation is His desire to fellowship with us. It is His design as it is ours. We were made to be like Him. As such, our attitude towards our friends should be like His. In Philippians 2:3-4, the apostle Paul states, *"Don't push your way to the front; don't sweet-talk your way to the top. Put yourself aside, and help others get ahead. Don't be obsessed with getting your own advantage. Forget yourselves long enough to lend a helping hand" (The Message).*

Friends have the ability to put one another before themselves. They point out instead of pointing to themselves. This can be very hard, as sometimes our friends do not love us back very well. But we are called to point out no matter what. Romans 12:10 says, *"Be good friends who love deeply; practice playing second fiddle" (The Message).*

Just as a healthy friend does not rescue us from our poor decisions, Jesus often does not interfere with the choices we make. But He does promise to experience our consequences and pain with us. A few verses down from our last passage, Romans 12:15 says, *"Rejoice with those who rejoice; mourn with those who mourn."*

If we all drove respectfully and carefully, we would not need speed limits. If we thought of others before ourselves, we would not need police officers to mediate and legislate for us. If we loved others more than we loved ourselves we would fulfill God's Law. This is exactly what Jesus did. God has given us friends to teach us, without obligation, to love others from the heart and give of ourselves within the context of connection. This kind of love is the fulfillment of the Law.

What a friend we have in Jesus. As He blesses us with friends, we have the opportunity to love the way He loves us and to learn more about His character as our friend. As this idea stirs within you, allow God to be your friend. Allow Him to sit with you in your sorrows and your joys. Speak with Him about your worries. Hang out with Him throughout the day. Invite Him to your parties and your family events. Let Him hang out with you as you cook a meal. He is a friend that will never fail you.

*The Least of These.* I've been in full-time ministry for many years. I think ministry often attracts those of us who want to help the "down and out" and bring some kind of hope to those who feel hopeless. This is a noble task. But sometimes I think it is easy for us to forget to whom Jesus is referring to when He speaks about "the least of these." More specifically, I forget that I am one of "the least of these."

In our tennis game of connection, God serves the ball by serving our deepest need: the salvation of our souls. Our salvation rests completely on His grace and goodness. Our ability to experience that grace and goodness depends on our willingness to walk onto the court and join God's game.

Some people are either not yet in the game, or they are so worn down they don't have the strength to play. Jesus called them "the least of these." His love is so amazing that He identifies with them completely.

God is a just, compassionate, and righteous God. As such, He sees the vulnerability and plight of our fallen state. He makes Himself equal to the child, the hungry, the thirsty, the homeless, the naked, the sick, and the imprisoned. Then He hides Himself within them and declares to His followers, "Come find me." Those of us who hear His voice are asked to bring His presence to those who can't experience Him yet, to the least of these. He tells us that the way we point to them is the same as we point to Him. In other words, when we serve them we are serving Him. This is how we hit the ball back.

At one point, we were the "least of these." We could not point to God for whatever reason. And while we were still sinners, trapped in our survival mindset, God pointed to us in Christ. Another follower of His, someone who wanted to point to God, pointed to you in your "least of these" place. Through someone's faithfulness to God, He saved you.

The abundant life requires that we live out the fellowship of the Trinity in this way. It is our design. When we can live from this place of focusing outside ourselves, God says His focus is drawn to us. We begin to look more like our original design. We begin to look more like Jesus as we pour our lives out as an offering for God to use ... we become usable. It is here that we connect to our oxygen supply, our Source, the breath of life.

Going Deeper

1. What relationship(s) come to mind when I ask you about what is hardest about relationships?
2. Pointing out is hard, especially if we do not know who will point back. What are you afraid no one will see if you do not point to yourself? What need or desire keeps pulling your focus to yourself?
3. What has your marriage, or your singleness, taught you about yourself and what keeps you from deep oneness with another?
4. What have you learned about yourself and your connection with God through the parent/child dynamic in your life? If your parents were less than honorable, what do you need to relearn?
5. How does the difference between power and authority impact your response to those in authority over you?
6. As Christ-followers, we are God's friends. In the day-to-day, what areas of your life do you need Jesus to show up as your friend?
7. As a "least of these," someone pointed to you. Who? And to whom are you pointing?

**5**

# The Power of Ownership:
## *Owning Our Separateness*

*"Symptoms are the voice of the soul."*
*David G. Benner*

*"God did not create sin, but He holds Himself*
*responsible for the possibility of sin, and the proof*
*that He does so is in the cross of our Lord Jesus*
*Christ." Oswald Chambers*

## THE CONNECTION GAME

In the sanctification process, there are three things we *can* do. Everything else is left for God to accomplish. We cannot change ourselves. We cannot save ourselves. We cannot fix our sin problem. But we can (say it with me) connect, we can own, and we can surrender.

We have learned that our task of connection calls for a pointing-out approach to others. Our design requires it. Made in the image of the ever-pointing-out God, pointing in goes against our very construction. Life is thwarted. Relationships die. Anger builds. Breathing stops. Healing, growth, change, hope, and the abundant life happen within the context of this pointing-out connecting. Connection is the game. If your spiritual life is not working, you are playing the wrong game.

If connection is the context, the court, then ownership is the ball. What is claimed is what is volleyed back and forth. In our relationship with God, we own what belongs to us (our sin, our talents, our dreams), and God owns what belongs to Him (His forgiveness, His gifts, His dreams for us). We own what is ours. God owns what is His.

The volley back and forth is surrender and submission. We submit our "stuff" to God, and He submits His back to us. We give Him our weakness. He gives us His strength. We give Him our fear. He gives us His peace. The process is continual, not a one-time event. Like breathing, the swapping of our lives for His life is an exchange of what we need to live abundantly for the toxic waste within us.

While we talk about connection, ownership, and surrender separately, they are as interconnected as our cardiovascular system. We can discuss individually how the lungs, the heart, and the veins work. But in real time they operate together. If one stops, the others stop as well. Similarly, connection, ownership, and surrender work intricately together in this process of living abundantly. We learn how to connect as we learn how to point outside of ourselves to others and to God. We own our design for intimacy. But true oneness requires autonomy as well. We must also own how we are separate. We own our separateness and surrender it to Him freely. Ownership is the powerful antidote to our bondage to sin.

## OWNERSHIP

Many years ago, I was involved in a car accident. I was with a friend in her car as she was driving. We were stopped at a light in the left turn lane behind a small pick-up truck. Without warning, a mini-van hit us from behind at about 35 mph, bending the frame of my friend's Jeep Cherokee.

We slammed into the truck in front of us, creating a double impact between my head and my headrest, leaving me with a mild concussion. At the same time, my seatbelt tightened in such a way that my back and hips were twisted out of alignment. I was in a lot of pain for a long time. The man driving the car that hit us was uninsured and unlicensed. He was driving the car illegally, and they took him away in a police car.

I did not cause this pain. I had not done anything wrong. The pain, however, was definitely mine. During that time of my life, I had to own my pain. I did not own the cause of my pain, just the pain itself. That ownership allowed me to take action to address it. Without ownership, I would have been waiting forever for the man who caused my suffering to fix it.

We often think of ownership in terms of property. Let's say you inherit a beach house. Some Uncle Bob, that you have never met, leaves it to you. Yeah! You enjoy it for several months before Hurricane Martha blows it to dust. Whose pile of rubble is it? Is it your fault? No, but it is your mess. That's ownership.

Here's another example: If I have a yard with a fence around it, my property lines are very clear. What is inside the fence is mine to address. If my neighbor throws his garbage into my yard, I have to address that. I may choose to throw it back over the fence. I may choose to simply clean it up. I may choose to sue my neighbor for constantly discarding his refuse on my lawn. But the point is that I have a choice if I own it. I don't own my neighbor's rude behavior. I don't take it in, as though it was mine. I simply own whatever is in my yard and address it appropriately.

Ownership also applies to all the things I have done. Some, if not much, of my pain has been caused by my own hand. My selfishness, my bitterness, and my unforgiveness have caused as much damage, if not more, than what anyone else could do to me. Sometimes my heart is the casualty of myself. Sometimes I am truly the victim of someone else's sin. Either way, heart damage is heart damage and I need healing.

So what about childhood abuse or being the victim of a crime? Ownership is more important than ever. But hear this clearly: we do not own what someone did to us. We never own someone else's sin. We do not deserve to be abused or assaulted or stolen from. We do not own that kind of shame. So what do we own?

We own the pain. We own the fear. We own the millions of ways we have tried to cope with the past. We own the isolation and the addictions. We own the passivity and the entitlement. We own the hundreds of ways we have tried to act independently of God to survive our past. We own the anger and the inability to trust that is left after such things. We own everything from our skin in. We may not have caused the struggle, but the struggle now belongs to us. The more we can appropriately own, the more choices we have, the more freedom we experience.

Ownership gives us power. It breaks the cord that ties us to the person who hurt us. Why is this important? We cannot surrender what we do not own. We cannot receive healing for anger we do not own. We cannot obtain the ability to trust if we never own our inability first. This is a step that cannot be skipped. Just like we cannot play tennis without the ball, we cannot surrender what we do not possess.

It is so easy for us to hide behind fear and blame. It is so simple to become passive and let life float past us. We often cling to the ways we cope—the numbness, the addictions, the busyness—to keep from owning what is in our hearts. It does not feel fair to own something we did not cause. In the next chapter, we will discuss at length how to forgive. But for this moment, let's explore the what. What do we need to own and release?

Here's a simple test: if you stop everything for a weekend, go away and have no responsibilities, what will come rushing up in your heart and mind? What does your busyness protect you from? What habits have you developed to keep from feeling negative emotions? What are your negative emotions? It is not the marriage, the job, or the financial situation that's keeping you from the abundant life. All the things you use to cope with the lack of abundance are holding you prisoner to a busy, unfulfilling life. You want to inhale God's goodness, but you haven't exhaled your noxious coping strategies in order to make room for Him. It's not the stuff on the outside that's hurting you. It is the stuff on the inside that you haven't owned yet, that you feel you have no choice about, that keeps you from experiencing God in His fullness.

Ownership is about taking stewardship over the inner life. It is about being more honest than ever before about how we cope with being fallen. If the Good News is really good, then we have nothing to fear. Our sin will be cleansed. Our anger will be healed. Our hearts will be made whole.

If someone else caused my pain, it is still my pain. If my beach house is in a big pile, it is my mess to deal with. If my yard is covered with leaves from my neighbor's tree, they are now my leaves. I may be angry with the person, the hurricane, the tree, or the neighbor. Anger is to be expected, but to stay in anger without making choices about what now belongs to me does not produce any positive result. When the pain is relational and I resolve to no longer trust anyone, I opt out of the game altogether. My pain reflects my need for connection with the Healer. In fact, it is my broken heart that makes me significant in God's Story. He came to bind broken hearts and set captives free.

We were made to need. We were made to be completely dependent on the provision and care of God. Our design requires connection and intimacy, and the ability to point outside ourselves. After Eden, all we have to offer is our brokenness, but owning our brokenness leads to our healing. Owning our weakness leads to strength. Owning our fear leads us to courage. What we own is what we surrender, and surrender is the stage on which God shows us who He is. He is Healer. He is Strength. He is Courage. This is His Story. God doesn't work from the outside to shape and form us. He works from the inside. He doesn't do His transforming work *to* us, but *through* us. We are active participants in this Story about making all things new, including you and me.

## TO VS. THROUGH

We often confuse perseverance with passivity. We interpret the idea of perseverance as a resentful waiting during times of suffering. The frustration level begins to build as the wait time increases with no change in our circumstances. As we passively "persevere" through our trials, problems begin to stack up, and we feel more and more trapped. We keep waiting for someone, something, or even God to do something **TO** us to make things change. We often fall into this pattern of victim thinking, feeling like the odds are never in our favor, and we cannot win at all.

We need to break that cycle, but we don't need another philosophical principle to do it. We need things to actually change for us. So to start, let's redefine the word perseverance. The Theological Dictionary of the New Testament defines it this way: *"courageous, active resistance to a hostile attack."* Both the apostle Paul (Romans 5:3-5) and James (James 1:2-4) tell us to rejoice when we suffer because such suffering produces perseverance (or endurance in other translations). At first glance, it appears that both Paul and James must be on a strong hallucinogen. How can suffering bring rejoicing? But both authors describe a process leading from suffering to hope. This process is activated through perseverance, our only healthy approach to suffering. All other coping strategies will fall short.

The word *perseverance* comes from the same root as the word *abide* in the Greek. It implies a sense of remaining and staying. It means not running away. To persevere is to stay in the truth, to remain in the feelings, to cling to God's goodness no matter what we see. When we choose to persevere, it allows God to do something **THROUGH** us in order to make things change. So how do we persevere? We learn the power of ownership.

Ownership is the practical side of the concept of perseverance that allows us to gain character through our suffering. Ownership means that whatever someone else has said or done to us is *NOT* ours, but what we choose to do next *IS* ours. If we want the abundant life, we must give up the blame game and accept that others cannot cause our feelings, reactions, or choices. With ownership, we are free to be who God has made us to be, free to really live. Ownership allows us to have self-control and dignity.

## THE POWER OF THE PROCESS

Paul beautifully outlines this process to hope:

> *And not only this, but we also exult in our tribulations, knowing that tribulation brings about perseverance; and perseverance, proven character; and proven character, hope; and hope does not disappoint, because the love of God has been poured out within our hearts through the Holy Spirit who was given to us (Romans 5:3-5).*

Suffering is always about disconnection. Suffering first entered our Story when we were separated (disconnected) from God in Eden, and the fruit of that disconnection continues on all human levels. We are disconnected from God and from others. What we know to be true (in our minds) and what we experience (in our hearts) are disconnected, leaving us disconnected even from ourselves.

Look back through the difficult experiences in your story. Do you notice how every moment of suffering came about because of some kind of separation? Maybe it was a divorce or the death of a loved one. Maybe it was the loss of a dream or your reputation. Childhood suffering can involve a separation from innocence or a parent's affection. Trauma brings about a disconnection from safety and the sense of security. Improperly addressed, the connection-designed human heart will scramble for safety. Finding none in its surroundings, it will go to isolation (becoming insulated from others and God) or addictions (to go numb and "cope" with the disconnect), but God's path is through perseverance.

Perseverance requires a sense of community. We cannot truly persevere alone. Therefore, if we are stuck in isolation or addictions, we are missing perseverance. Perseverance is suffering with perspective. Our perspective must reflect God's transcendent Story instead of simply focusing on our own pain. It is not passively waiting, but actively standing in the truth. We remain with what is ours so we can offer it in surrender. We stop excusing our behavior and justifying our actions. We stop the blame game and start focusing on what we can do instead of what someone else is supposed to do. We end the defensive, self-protective approach of speck removal for others and focus on the logs in our own eyes.

As we begin to take ownership of what is ours, a shift happens within, and everything changes. As we clear out our entitled thinking and resentful feelings, we make a space for deep relationships. As we offer what is in our hearts to our Healer, we can begin to own His attributes within us as we breathe out our toxins and breathe in His presence. As we remain in truth, we begin to see love, joy, peace, and patience develop within us. Ownership allows us to make room in our hearts for that flood of love, the deep connection that God has offered to us. This kind of perseverance leads us to proven character.

Character equals the attributes we have to contribute to relationship. Character means nothing to a hermit, as it is only meaningful within the context of interpersonal relationships. We use words like honesty, integrity, and trustworthiness to describe it.

As I own my anger or pain or sadness, God can work through me to begin to shift what my experience is on the inside. As He clears out the anger, pain, or sadness, I gain more space for relationship. What I own I can surrender. What I claim as mine, I can offer up. If I do not own what is mine, I suffer from either passivity or entitlement. If I believe that I am always a victim, I will miss the transformation that Jesus has for me. I will miss hope. While I cannot really change what I own, I can offer it to God for healing. Through this character-building healing of my broken (disconnected) heart, I find hope.

Hope is deep, experiential connection with God. It is the familiarity and understanding of God's love being poured into our hearts. When I think of hope, I think of a television show called *Extreme Makeover: Home Edition*. Each episode depicts an actual family in desperate need who gets a completely new home in place of their current, run-down shack-for-a-house. At the end of each show, the host and the family stand in front of a giant bus blocking the view of their new house. Bursting with excitement and expectation, the family waits for the signal. In one voice the entire crowd yells, "Bus Driver…MOVE THAT BUS!" As the bus pulls away and the new house is revealed, the expressions on the family's faces show us what hope feels like.

Years ago, there was a lab rat study that demonstrated the need for hope. A rat was put into a bowl of water, without the ability to get out, and left there to swim, until it drowned eleven hours later. The next rat was put in the same water but was pulled out at ten hours. When put back in, it made if for fourteen hours. When rescued again, and placed the next day in the water, it made it for sixteen hours. Why? Because it was able to endure something as long as it knew it wasn't going to last forever.

Hope is the assurance that our suffering won't be forever. We can persevere because it's only for now. We can own all that is in our hearts because it can all be healed and cleansed. Jesus said that He went to prepare a mansion for us. One day in heaven, we will say with Him, "MOVE THAT BUS!" and we will see that everything will be okay forever. No more bills. No more pain. No more crying. No more betrayal. No more disconnection. Ever.

WHAT IS MINE?

So how do we start this ownership process? And what exactly do we own? Allow the Holy Spirit to teach you what is truly yours. Here are some guiding thoughts as you explore it with Him. Ask yourself the following questions:

- What are the themes of my thoughts when I'm stressed? What do I tell myself when things are not going well?
- Am I often angry? About what? Are there themes?
- Am I often depressed and hopeless?
- Do I seek revenge, even if only in my thought life? Do I often have imaginary conversations where I tell people off and put them in their places?
- If I am more honest with myself than I've ever been, what am I most afraid of? When I ask that question, what pops into my head first, before the filter kicks in?

The following are some areas of life that require ownership and attention. Take some time to think, journal, or simply pray about each one:

*Thoughts.* Every thought I have is mine. Someone may influence how I think, or the content of the thought, but it is my thought if it is in my head.

*Feelings.* My feelings are not facts; they are signals telling me about what I actually believe. Like the gaslight on the car, they tell me that I need to pay attention to something important. Because I am responsible for how I act on those feelings, I must own them.

*Attitudes and Perspectives.* My vantage point is just that: mine. I may be at a good angle to accurately assess the situation, or I may not. I may be right. I may not have enough information. I cannot claim to be the only authority on what is true, and so I own just how I see it, without claiming that how I see it is how it is.

*Words.* If I say something, my words are mine. My tone of voice is mine.

*Intentions.* If I strip away my rationalization and lawyer tricks, I must honestly ask myself what I mean by my actions.

*My Sin.* Most people, even those who do not walk with God, know they sin. But we live in a culture that no longer acknowledges sin as a problem. The "we're only human" defense can only go so far and it leaves us locked out of the abundant life we crave.

We need to get honest about our sin, not to wallow, but to persevere. We don't want to escape the responsibility of our sin by blaming or choosing to do nothing about it. Instead, we want to own what is ours so God can change things through us. Sometimes owning our sin is very painful. We don't want to admit that we are capable of such things. Sometimes we don't even know we are sinning. We move through life and hit the same roadblocks, over and over again, but don't deduce that we are actually in a pattern of sin. Sin is pervasive and often subtle, but it keeps us from experiencing all the fruit of the Spirit we crave in our lives. We are freed from sin through confession.

Confession is nothing more than agreeing with the truth. Think about a courtroom. When the accused says, "I did it," he is simply agreeing with the accusation. When God, through His Word or a whisper says, "This is sin," He is asking us to agree with Him. Sometimes the agreeing brings yucky feelings, but we are called to persevere through them, not run away. Biblical perseverance always happens within the context of truth. We remain in the truth instead of blaming, minimizing, isolating, or escaping. When we confess, we own what we have done.

*Needs.* God asks that we ask. He does not promise *how* He will answer or *when*, but God offers that when we come to Him in proactive dependence, we will always find Him, and He will always answer.

*Gifts.* Have you ever done a jigsaw puzzle and discovered there was one piece missing? Or have you put a new desk together only to find that the last screw that holds the fourth leg in place is not in the package? Can you imagine if our human bodies did the same thing? What if there were missing pieces? What if we could lose a thyroid gland, just misplace it? What happens to us if any part of our bodies stops working? We consider ourselves to be sick.

The Bible states clearly that as Christians we make up a body. If we decide to be passive about our membership in the body of Christ, everyone suffers. When we do not accept the calling to take our place under the Headship of Jesus, we are missing the connection and community God has for us. While we may not feel like we belong anywhere, we definitely do belong in Christ's Body. If we don't *know* where we fit, that's one thing. If we don't *choose* to fit, that is another. If we don't know our place in the body of Christ, we can find it by looking at what makes us come alive. What do you do that ignites a holy passion within you? There is a place for everyone. When we do not step up and own our part in the body of Christ, it is as though a part of His body stops working. It makes God's church sick. We need every piece in our puzzle.

*Desires.* C.S. Lewis, in his address entitled *The Weight of Glory*, writes, "If we consider the unblushing promises of reward and the staggering nature of the rewards promised in the Gospels, it would seem that Our Lord finds our desires not too strong, but too weak."

The apostle John tells a story of a man who was paralyzed. Everyday this man was taken to the pool of Bethesda to wait for healing. Apparently, an angel would come from time to time and stir the waters there. When this happened, the first person to get in the pool would be healed. Day after day, this man was dragged there to try to be the first one in. After 38 years, longer than Jesus had been on the earth as a human, this man faithfully pursued his healing. Jesus asked him an amazing question: "Do you wish to get well?" Um … duh? Do you wish to get well? OF COURSE he wants to get well. Why would he do this if he didn't want to get well? But it is an excellent question. What happens if he gets well? What will he do with his life if he doesn't have to go down to the pool every day? It begs the same question of us: What will we do if we get what we want? I think Jesus asks us the same question. It's hard to answer. We are afraid to get what we want, and we're afraid that we won't get what we want.

Jesus owned what He wanted as well. In the garden of Gethsemane, Jesus asked the Father to take the cup of His death away from Him. He was anxious to the point of sweating blood. Even though Jesus did not get what He wanted, He owned His desire and offered it to the Father.

When we own what we want, we can offer it to God. God will either grant it or change us to align with His desires for us. Jesus had to ask three times before He could truly surrender, but He never gave up His desire. We are not called to squash our desires, just surrender them. But before we can surrender anything, we must claim it as ours. Jesus asks us the same question: "What do you want?"

## GOD'S EXAMPLE

When my brother got married, he and his wife lit the unity candle as part of their ceremony. As they lit the center candle, they did not extinguish their individual candles when setting them back in their original places. Both my brother and sister-in-law had the wisdom to know that unity requires separateness, not enmeshment. This is a good example of our relationship with God. While we have been created in God's image, we are not God. He is separate from us even though He has made Himself one with us. While He became one of us, He is also very different from us.

God is clear that He is far above us, and the property lines that He sets help us to know what belongs to us and what belongs to Him. He owns His thoughts, feelings, and actions toward us, and His choices on our behalf. He is clear that our sin belongs to us, and yet He owns His choice to allow sin in the first place. In the same way that God owns His choices, He asks us to own ours. This ownership reflects a maturity that comes with an attitude of pointing out rather than pointing to self. God is the definition of character.

Early in my walk with God my friends and I would say, "If God said it then it is written into the fabric of the universe!" God always owns what He says He will do. Nowhere is this more tangible than in the area of forgiveness. While God never owned the choices of His first creations, He did own His feelings of betrayal and hurt. He never took credit for my sin either, but He has owned His decision to provide the way for me to point to Him. God is our example of ownership. What an amazing leader He is!

Going Deeper

1.  What event in your past keeps you stuck now?
2.  Suffering is always about disconnection. How do you avoid feeling disconnected? Is it isolation? Some habit or addiction?
3.  Both Paul and James tell us to rejoice in our sufferings. What do they mean? (See Romans 5:3-5 and James 1:2-4).
4.  Is there a theme to the grudges you hold? Do you feel unimportant? Disrespected? Persecuted?
5.  Character equals the attributes we have that contribute to relationship. List character traits that fit this description. Can negative character traits also contribute to relationships...negatively?
6.  Have you ever experienced real hope? What was it like?
7.  Of the long list of things we own, which are the most difficult for you?

# 6
# Forgiveness:
# *Owning Our Hearts*

*"One of the greatest challenges of the spiritual life
is to receive God's forgiveness." Henri Nouwen*

*"Whoever defends himself will have himself for his
defense, and he will have no other. But let him come
defenseless before the Lord and he will have for his
defender no less than God Himself." A.W. Tozer*

*"The trouble with steeling yourself against the
harshness of reality is that the same steel that
secures your life against being destroyed secures
your life also against being opened up and transformed by the holy power that life itself comes from.
You can survive on your own. You can grow strong
on your own. You can prevail on your own. But you
cannot become human on your own."
Frederick Buechner*

One day when I was about nine or ten years old, my mother
was having a very difficult day. I don't remember the
details except that I knew she was exhausted and discour-
aged. Strategizing to win the daughter-of-the-year award (as

the only girl in the family), I decided I would offer to do the dishes after dinner. I was preparing my amazing speech that would leave my mother crying from the sheer beauty of the offer. My plan: to eat my last bite and announce my considerate and sacrificial gift to the entire table. As I was chewing that last bite, avoiding talking with my mouth full, my mother turned to me and asked, "Gina, will you please do the dishes for me?"

My bubble burst, and I began to cry. Lacking the skills of a more mature person, I protested that I did not want to do the dishes—a response that lost me the coveted award I had in the bag a few moments earlier. I had been planning to do the dishes. What was the big deal? Well, it was obviously not my choice anymore. I was no longer able to give from a "giving place," but instead had to proceed out of obligation.

Boundaries are what protect the giving place. Boundaries give us the option of saying no, so that we can freely say yes. Boundaries are property lines that determine ownership. They determine where we need to mow and who is the owner of a felled tree. In relationships, boundaries are the defining property lines for ownership as well. We have discussed ownership in the context of the negative emotions and experiences "within our skin," but we also own the good stuff as well. This includes love, trust, generosity, innocence, peace, joy, and the like. When the good stuff is taken rather than given, a debt occurs. What is taken can no longer be offered because it is gone. This debt needs to be forgiven.

Forgiveness was originally a money term. When someone owes something but is unable to pay it back, they need their debt to be forgiven. When someone violates a boundary, they need forgiveness as well. When someone has taken from us, God is asking us to for*give*. He wants us to choose to give after the fact. If we don't forgive, we are trapped in the bitterness and resentment that remains, and we are forced to point to ourselves to get back what was taken.

## THE PURPOSE OF FORGIVENESS

In Matthew 18, Jesus tells a story about a rich king who decided to settle his accounts with his slaves. One man owed the king ten thousand talents. A talent was worth about fifteen years' salary, so to owe ten thousand was outrageous. Jesus, in essence, was saying this man owed a gazillion dollars without the means to pay it back. After being thrown in debtor's prison, this slave begged and pleaded with the king and actually received forgiveness for his debt. Understand this meant that the king was out ten thousand talents.

Later, the same man decided to settle his accounts with a fellow slave. This other man owed the first man one hundred denarii, or about one hundred day's wages. Furious that the indebted man could not pay, the forgiven slave had his friend thrown into the same debtor's prison from which he had just been released, refusing to forgive the debt. When the king learned of this, he was enraged. In his anger, the king renounced the forgiveness of the slave and turned him over to the "torturers" until the entire debt was paid.

The king pointed to his slave in mercy, and the slave pointed to himself. The king then pointed to his slave with justice. When God points to us, it is with a finger of mercy. When we are pointing with mercy, we reflect Him. When we point to ourselves or to others with judgment, God will point with justice. We don't want His justice pointed in our direction. We do not want to receive what we deserve.

At the end of this passage, Jesus makes a very strong statement. He says that His Father will turn us over for judgment if we do not forgive each other from the heart. Forgiveness is the ultimate test of our true transformation. If we do not forgive, we are not reflecting our God-image. God forgives. Every time. Seventy times seven. It is His kindness that leads us to repentance, not His constant attempts to prove that we are wrong.

When people have wronged us, we want them exposed in the light. We want justice. We want the scales to be tipped back in our favor. No one really enjoys being a victim, and when we have been wronged, we want the spotlight to shine. But we must be willing to stand under the same light. If we are hurt by someone's rage, for example, then our anger-driven rant leaves us as guilty as the one who raged against us. Punching someone because we have been punched leaves us guilty too. Judge not lest you be judged.

During the 2009 Super Bowl, a commercial aired for a Tide brand stain remover. In this ad, a man was trying to interview for a job but had a huge stain on his shirt. As he tried to speak and impress his interviewer, the stain would speak in mumbled nonsense louder than the man's voice. Completely distracted by the obnoxious stain, the interviewer was obviously perplexed and did not comprehend a word the man was trying to say, as impressive as he tried to be.

When we walk in unforgiveness and then try to pray, the stain on our hearts speaks so loudly that God does not hear our requests for mercy and forgiveness. When we refuse to forgive, it means that someone else's sin has stained our hearts. Do you want to carry a stain from someone else's sin? We forgive so that our hearts are clean. We forgive so that another's transgressions do not determine our ability to stay connected with God through our pointing out design. Forgiveness is the ultimate boundary.

## UNDERSTANDING PUNISHMENT

When we have been hurt, we want to punish. This is basic fallen-human nature. Think about it: if someone cuts you off in traffic, what do you want to do? If, after standing in line for 3000 minutes at Disney World and the ride closes, what does your attitude reflect? Punishment says, "You will pay for what you've done!" We want people to pay us back for the hurt, the embarrassment, the devastation, the innocence that was taken. We want them to get what they deserve.

This often-intense drive within us reflects something important: we need justice. Think about when you were a five-year-old, and your older sister got more ice cream than you. THAT'S NOT FAIR. We've always needed balanced scales. We set up government systems and pay lots of money for people to play the role of impartial judge to gain a sense of justice. Our need for justice is a good thing. God is just. Our drive for justice reflects our image-bearing similarity to our Creator.

But as fallen people, we want revenge. We don't want our offender to get away with the offense, and so we hold the grudge. We fear that if we forgive, then someone gets away with sin. That's not fair. That's not just.

But our means of accomplishing justice and God's means are very different. God handles justice distinctly His own way. He is clear about the need for punishment, but rather than impose it on the offender, God has taken it upon Himself. Remember the king from our story at the beginning of this chapter? When his slave owed him the ten thousand talents, he forgave the debt, leaving himself with a deficit of ten thousand talents. The king absorbed the punishment for the slave. God has absorbed our punishment. He paid for what we have done. He is then asking us to act like Him toward others.

God is perfectly just, and He is perfectly merciful. He is both at the same time. The cross is the intersection where these two qualities meet. My debt and yours were paid, but not by you and me. Justice happened, but mercy happened simultaneously. Only God could pull off such a thing. Seriously. Only God could do that. So how does He expect us to follow His example?

## UNDERSTANDING GOD'S PROVISION

Forgiveness is the fundamental test of faith. When we have been wronged, we will either act like our Creator or we won't. Do we trust that God is good and that He will provide what we need? This is when being a Christian means something. This is no longer a drill. This is real time, real life, rubber-meets-the-road Christianity. Forgiveness does not concern those who want their own way. Those of us who wrestle to forgive someone are those who want the abundant life and don't want to settle for any substitutes of simple survival. This is when faith matters.

But I don't know what you've been through, right? I don't know what he did. I don't know how badly she hurt you. I don't see the depth of the betrayal. I don't know how many times someone has done this to you without remorse. I don't know how unique your situation is and how forgiveness can't possibly apply to your situation. Somehow, you have the right to your stain. I understand. I have felt pain like that, too. And so has God.

When Adam and Eve grabbed the forbidden fruit and took the fateful bite, God knew what it felt like to be wronged. He understood betrayal. He understood how it felt to not be enough for someone. He felt the despair. By the sixth chapter of Genesis, God declared that He was sorry He even made mankind. Throughout His Story, God's people have consistently betrayed, blamed, and even hated Him. God says He despises lying. His people lie all the time. He states that He hates idolatry. We worship money, time, and our own needs with reckless abandonment. He tells us to forgive, and we hold grudges. He understands what it is like when the people who are supposed to love Him don't act in loving ways. The very people He came to save killed Him. The people that He healed and fed cried out for Barabbas to be freed so that He could be crucified. And yet, after the torture (literally) and through the excruciating pain, He asked the Father to forgive them. What kind of love is this?

It is a love that we cannot possess without the Lover. It is an attribute of God that we don't get without Him, without His presence in us. We cannot forgive outside our connection to the God of forgiveness. Because He has forgiven you ten thousand talents, He is asking you to forgive the one hundred denarii. Own the debt. You didn't create it, but own what is in your skin.

As we own what is ours and offer it to our Source, He makes up the difference. In the book of Joel, God tells a story about a massive army of locusts. The book starts with an announcement about what happened. God declares, through His prophet Joel that swarms of locusts came and destroyed all the crops of the Israelites. What the gnawing locusts left, the swarming locusts ate. What the swarming locusts left, the creeping locusts ate. And what the creeping locusts left, the stripping locusts ate. There was nothing left. Everything was taken.

We turn the page in the story and read God's response to His people in Joel 2:25. God states that He will restore the years that the swarming, creeping, stripping, and gnawing locusts have eaten. *He* will make up the years that were taken. God did not promise to have a long talk with the locusts and make them bring back what they took. He did not tell the Israelites to suck it up and move ahead. He promised to provide and restore what was taken. He promises us the same thing. Without this promise, we cannot forgive. Because of this promise, we are required to forgive. God understands that sin is contagious. When someone sins against us, and we want justice, we will sin to try to get it. He tells us that vengeance belongs to Him, and He will repay. We are to trust Him to restore the years that were taken.

With this in mind, we can approach the process of forgiveness. Within the context of our game of connection with

God, we will be able to work through this practice of forgiving to keep the stain of another's sin off our hearts. Let's begin ...

## STEP ONE: NAMING THE WOUND

Our first step in forgiveness addresses the questions of who and what. Who needs forgiveness and for what offense? Have you ever blamed someone for something someone else did? Have you ever blamed God for the sin of a parent? Or blamed a parent for the sin of a sibling? You are in good company. Eve blamed a snake for her sin, and Adam blamed Eve and God for his. We must see a clear picture of whom we need to forgive; otherwise, we spend years angry and bitter against someone who had no power to change the situation.

Once we have established the person(s), we must become clear about the offense. What happened? Describe the event. Name the transgression. We forgive actions, things that were done. We don't forgive character flaws. We don't forgive a person for always being lazy. We forgive him for the seventy times he has proven his laziness through actions. We name the event that we are forgiving. We trace the loss back to a specific incident.

Usually this event caused a wound because something was taken: safety, money, health, or something that is difficult or impossible to get back. Once we know the root cause of the wound, we must name the wound itself. What is the debt? What was taken? We must name it honestly without over exaggeration or minimizing. What value did the taken thing hold? In order to forgive, we must be clear about what we are forgiving. If you steal five dollars from me, my reaction will be different than if you steal five hundred thousand dollars from me.

Forgiving a parent's abuse is about naming the painful events that left you empty, afraid, alone, and unable to trust. Forgiving an ex-spouse requires identifying exactly what happened, on both sides, and placing the appropriate value on what was lost. Forgiving children and friends requires the same authentic naming. We do not sugarcoat these events but name them honestly. If we are to truly forgive and move forward, we must count the cost of what was lost.

The following is a chart that can help with this step of letting the event stand as history:

| Who hurt me? | What happened that hurt me? What did I lose? | What value did this loss have to me? |
|---|---|---|
| | | |
| | | |
| | | |
| | | |
| | | |

If needed, grab a piece of paper and make a chart like this one, making it as long and detailed as necessary. The more authentic we are with this exercise, the more authentic our forgiveness and the deeper the healing. You may need to spend some time with it. Just own what you write down. Own your hurt. Own the value of what was lost. Own the anger and the feelings of betrayal. Own so you can offer them to the One who can heal them.

God does this. He is very clear about our sin. The Ten Commandments spell out in precise detail what God is asking from us. When confronting His people, God always gives specific examples of where and when they strayed from Him. During this step, we allow the anger, the pain, and the grief to surface. We uncover the stain left by someone else so it can be cleansed and no longer taint our hearts.

## STEP TWO: TAKE OWNERSHIP OF OUR EMOTIONAL RESPONSES

This is very difficult. Let's get some Biblical perspective on this idea. Galatians 6: 1-2 states:

> *Brethren, even if anyone is caught in any trespass, you who are spiritual, restore such a one in a spirit of gentleness; each one looking to yourself, so that you too will not be tempted. Bear one another's burdens, and thereby fulfill the law of Christ.*

Paul, in his letter to the Galatians, is asking us (we who are spiritual) to rise above the sin of another and respond with gentleness.

When you read this, what images of God come to mind? We tend to project our own thoughts and feeling onto God and how He would react. This is subtle, but let's say the spouse of a close family member was just caught in an affair. You are angry. You are hurt. A million feelings surface. Someone hands you a Bible, opens it to this passage, and you read. What is your initial response?

Mine would not be gentleness toward the person who cheated on my family member or the person who handed me the Bible. I don't want to look at myself in those moments; I want to focus on the one who caused these bad feelings and find a way to punish.

Believe it or not, this passage is for the safety and edification of the wronged person. Let's break it down. Paul states that when someone has sinned, our goal is to be restoration instead of revenge. The drive for vengeance is the temptation. The strong desire to assume the role of judge and pronounce a sentence will lead us to our own sin if we give in to that desire. Our hearts cannot stay clean in a mud fight. Getting even does not solve things; it makes us as dirty as the one who threw the first mud clod. Just a few verses before this passage Paul outlines the fruit of the Spirit (Galatians 5:22-23). Self-control ends the list. If someone has lost self-control, it does not excuse me losing mine. Paul states that I need to look at myself. If my friend offends me and falls off a cliff, I need to watch myself instead of following after.

Paul then tells us to bear each other's burdens and thus fulfill the law of Christ. What is the burden, and what is the law of Christ? The word for burden here implies something that is too much for one person. If someone sins against me, the impact of that sin on me is more than he can assume. He can't fix it. He can't take it back. It's done. That burden becomes mine. I am to bear that burden and thus fulfill the law of Christ, to bear the sins of others. Isn't that what Christ did?

This is not a command in the sense of, "You'll be in trouble young lady if you don't do this!" Rather, this is an invitation to walk with Jesus and suffer the way He suffered. This is an invitation to the very life of Christ Himself. He is asking us to remain connected to Him by acting like Him when others sin against us. He bears the burden of our sins. He does not require that we fix it or make it up to Him. He knows we cannot, and so He bears the relational burden that we set on Him. He is asking us to do the same. Let's continue with the passage. Galatians 6: 3-5 states:

*For if anyone thinks he is something when he is nothing, he deceives himself. But each one must examine his own work, and then he will have reason for boasting in regard to himself alone, and not in regard to another. For each one will bear his own load.*

How smug we can become when someone wrongs us. How quickly we can justify our sinful reactions to someone's sin and somehow feel superior as we do it. This is the stain of unforgiveness. This is the contagious nature of sin. God is asking us to own our emotional responses so that we do not fall into the same pit as the offender. When someone sins against me, I am still responsible for myself. Comparing the degree of my reaction to the degree of the offense does not keep the stain off my heart. Rather than allowing another's sin to define my response, I must ask myself, "Who do I want to be in this situation?" Just because I am bearing the sin burden of another does not give me the ability to drop my own load.

So what does this word "load" mean? The word was used to describe the packs that soldiers would wear to carry their things. My load is everything I am responsible for. My load is what I own. Interestingly, this is the same word (translated here as 'burden') used in Matthew 11:30 when Jesus says, "My yoke is easy and my burden [load] is light."

When the load that we carry becomes heavy because of the burden of sin from someone else, we can trade it for Christ's light load. When anger, hurt, and pain overwhelm us and the load gets heavy, we can exchange it for the light burden that Jesus is offering.

Now let me be clear about something. When we bear the sin burden for someone, the sin burden is the impact the sin has had on us. We bear the impact (the loss, the pain, etc.) but we do NOT bear the sin. That is God's job. We do not become doormats in the name of bearing burdens. If we allow people to continually sin against us, we become accomplices to their sin. We are to restore them, not excuse them. Forgiveness is not resignation. Forgiveness is the perfect amalgamation of mercy and justice. We do not abandon justice for the sake of mercy. We bear the justice for the sake of mercy. So how do we do that? Let's move to step three.

## STEP THREE: DON'T STOP BREATHING

We have identified the who and the what. We have owned our emotional responses, carried the burden of sin, and carried our own loads. But the debt still remains. Something valuable is missing. How does God restore the years that have been taken? How can God restore the pieces of life that have been devastated? Every good workout instructor will, at some point in the session, tell you to keep breathing. Physical endurance requires the release of carbon dioxide and the intake of oxygen. Our endurance through the forgiveness process looks much the same way. God gives us some principles to guide us as we continue in our passage. Galatians 6:7-10:

> *Do not be deceived, God is not mocked; for whatever a man sows, this he will also reap. For the one who sows to his own flesh will from the flesh reap corruption, but the one who sows to the Spirit will from the Spirit reap eternal life. Let us not lose heart in doing good, for in due time we will reap if we do not grow weary. So then, while we have opportunity, let us do good to all people, and especially to those who are of the household of the faith.*

If I want to grow tomatoes, I had better plant tomatoes. I cannot manipulate God or get out of the consequences of this harvest by blaming the clerk at the seed store or boycotting gardening altogether. I will reap what I sow. This is a principle that God designed to work on every level, a natural law in all areas of life.

If I react to another's sin with vengeance, malice, self-serving manipulation, or slander, I will not enjoy the harvest of my actions. If the only seeds being offered by the offender are the like, I don't want what is presented. I need to cancel my requirements that the offender pay me back for the sin burden I am bearing. I do not want the offender to be my seed supplier. I do not want my reactions to be determined by someone who would so offend me. But I still need what was taken during the wrongdoing.

So I must sow in the Spirit rather than the flesh. What does this mean? It means that I engage in the game of connection, own all the hurt, pain, anger, and fear, and throw it all onto God's side of the net. I surrender in humility before Him and ask Him to restore what was taken. I stop looking for the offender to fix how I feel. I stop requiring the offender to change so I can behave more appropriately. I stop making the offender my source for healing. Otherwise, in some strange way, my offender becomes my idol, and I stop depending on God, my true Source. I make this story about me, and my hurt and my desires. I point to me instead of the Lover of my soul. I do not want that harvest. Do you?

When we allow God to restore what was taken, He graciously works the harvest principle in our favor. If we do not give up, we will receive a wonderful harvest. If we do not grow weary, but continue owning and offering the debt, He will bless the seeds and the return will be abundant. He says so. And in God's Story, when He speaks things happen.

We know the quality of gold by testing it with fire. We know what a Christian is made of by how he or she handles forgiveness. We will either look like our Creator or we won't. Forgiveness requires the deepest wisdom and the strongest courage to own what is ours and not own what belongs to the offender. This wisdom and courage does not happen through our own power. We do not get these attributes of God without Him. He must be present with us to do this. In forgiveness, we must play the connection game well. We must understand how to point out, even when it hurts. We must understand what is ours and how to own it. And we must learn the volley of surrender.

## FORGIVENESS VS RECONCILIATION

We often assume that forgiveness and reconciliation are the same thing. They are not. While they are connected in many ways, forgiveness does not always lead to reconciliation. Forgiveness requires one person. Reconciliation requires two people or more. This is how we can forgive someone who has died, even if we never reconcile. This is how God could forgive us two thousand years ago without our participation. Forgiveness focuses on paying off a debt. Reconciliation focuses on restoring a relationship.

Therefore, forgiveness is required for reconciliation. Reconciliation, however, is not required for forgiveness. The Bible makes it clear that forgiveness is required for every offense. Reconciliation cannot happen if the offender is not willing to repent. In other words, we can forgive someone but not be reconciled if they refuse to stop offending. We forgive "seventy times seven" for every offense, but often from a distance. We are not required to subject ourselves to abuse or sinful behavior from someone in the name of forgiveness. Romans 12:18 states, *"If possible, so far as it depends on you, be at peace with all men."* If possible. God is leaving room for the other person to choose to remain in sin. If God does not hold you responsible for fixing someone's sin problem, then why should you?

Reconciliation requires repentance. The offender's heart must change for the relationship to be restored. While we were forgiven when Jesus died for us, we were not reconciled to God until we owned our sin and repented. We had to turn away from the heart attitude of defining our own right and wrong and acknowledge our offenses toward God. This is how we entered the connection game. We began to point out instead of pointing to ourselves. Reconciliation requires the same pointing out among our fellow humans.

Forgiveness comes first, then we are freed to reconcile. Without forgiveness, the process of reconciliation is tainted.

We think we are reconciling but really we are trying to hold the offender close, under the guise of forgiving them, trying to make them pay for what they have done. We use sometimes subtle, sometimes blatant guilt, manipulation, and fear tactics to punish. This is not forgiveness or reconciliation. Justice is the price for mercy. We pay for the justice ourselves and offer the mercy to the one who caused the debt.

## RECEIVING GOD'S FORGIVENESS

This is exactly what God has done for us. God has amazing property lines. He is very clear about what belongs to Him and what is ours. As a result, His giving place is secure. He can offer Himself completely to us, and He does. When we offend Him, He chooses His emotional responses. His kindness leads us to repentance. His mercy woos us to Him. He decides who He will be to us. His name is Wonderful, Strength, Loving, Forgiving, Peace, Mercy, and hundreds more. He does not depend on our ability to stop sinning to determine how His day is going. He is free.

As we receive His forgiveness and His example, we share in His freedom. The sin from someone else does not stain our hearts. An offender's inability or unwillingness to stop sinning no longer determines our well-being.

God is not asking us to do something that He has not done and that He is not willing to do through us. Own what is in your heart. Own all the good, the bad, and the ugly. Own the pain and the joy. Own the wounds so you can own the healing. Ownership is your ticket to the freedom and abundance that you so desperately need. Forgiveness is the ultimate exercise in ownership.

Going Deeper

1. What impact has unforgiveness had in your life?
2. If you are honest, can you trust that God will make up the difference for what someone else has taken?
3. Can we really forgive ourselves? Why or why not?
4. As you work through the chart, what feelings come to the surface? Can you sit with them or do you find yourself skipping that part?
5. God wants us to forgive for our sake. What stain, from someone else's sin, are you still carrying?
6. We know what a Christian is made of by how he or she handles forgiveness. What are you made of?
7. Is there anyone in your life that you can forgive, but with whom you may not be able to reconcile? How do you know reconciliation is not possible?

# Surrendering...

- to give up possession of or power over; yield to another
- to give up claim to; give over or yield, especially voluntarily as in favor of another
- to give up oneself to another's power and control

*"Jesus invites us to thirst. Satan invites us to control through performance of one kind or another." Brent Curtis and John Eldredge*

*"If we cooperate with him in loving obedience, God will manifest himself to us, and that manifestation will be the difference between a nominal Christian life and a life radiant with the light of his face." A.W. Tozer*

We often think of surrender as a powerless resignation to someone who is forcing us against our wills. We think of armies who are outnumbered or Circle K employees at gunpoint. But Biblical surrender is the practice of exchange. We trade our stuff for God's in an exhale/inhale motion. And we do this by choice. In fact, without making the choice to surrender, nothing changes. God never forces us to do anything.

# 7
# Trust and Obey:
## *Surrendering Through Faith*

*"Faith is the gaze of a soul upon a saving God."*
*A.W. Tozer*

*"There is a virtuous fear which is the effect of faith,*
*and a vicious fear which is the product of doubt and*
*distrust. The former leads to hope relying on God,*
*in whom we believe; the latter inclines to despair,*
*as not relying on God." Blaise Pascal*

*"Faith makes, life proves, trials confirm, and death*
*crowns the Christian." John George Christian*
*Hopfner*

S ir Isaac Newton is said to have discovered gravity, but
really he just named it. Gravity is a natural law that has
always been true. We can count on it. It is unchangeable. We
wish we could adjust the effects sometimes because gravity
does terrible things to our bodies over time, and it determines the number on the scale in the morning. But gravity
just is. We don't think about it. We just walk this planet with
our feet on the ground and never acknowledge that gravity
allows us to do just that.

In the same way, God has also created spiritual laws. There are certain principles that, when understood, hold our lives together. If we try to defy gravity we will, at some point (possibly painfully), end up back on the ground. If we try to defy God's spiritual laws, we will end up in bondage to sin. Just as gravity holds our feet to the ground, faith and obedience hold our hearts to the fellowship of the Trinity and the abundant life.

Imagine if gravity stopped working. Birds couldn't land. Bodies of water would float away, killing all the fish. Our muscles would atrophy from the lack of resistance. The plus side: we could all fly, and no one would have a weight problem. The downside: we would have to develop an entirely new way to survive. We depend on gravity as a basic assumption, a hard-wired reality that makes our lives work.

When our first parents ate from the tree of the knowledge of good and evil, they no longer trusted their Father. They questioned His motives. They sought to independently decide their own course. What came naturally to them before became a foreign concept to them after. As a result, everything was flipped upside down. Now, for us, trusting God is our last resort instead of our first impulse. But it was never meant to be this way. Maybe this is why Jesus told us to come to Him as a child. Children understand how to trust and obey.

As adults, however, do we truly trust anyone? And don't we feel we have outgrown the need to obey? How do we trust a God who allows terrible things to happen and whose 911 responses take a really long time? Sure, He'll help you find your car keys, but God didn't keep your marriage from falling apart, or your child away from the wrong influences, or the bank from calling the loan.

It is hard to trust anyone in such a violent world. While we were born with a certain level of innocence, it was quickly stripped away by both the outside world and our inner fallen nature. As a result, the Christian life is not natural to us at all. We have been living apart from gravity in a gravity-grounded world. If we truly want to live the abundant life, (not some cheap substitute that is labeled 'Christian' but seeks only to manage behavior), we must ground ourselves in God's spiritual laws. Faith and obedience are all we have to keep us from floating away from this abundant life.

WHAT IS FAITH?

If we took a video camera on the street and asked people about their faith, we would get some interesting answers. We would hear that some people are Baptists or that they grew up as Methodists. Some would tell us they do not really do the church thing or they try to be good people. Still others would be different religions like Muslim or Buddhist. "Tell me about your faith," translates into, "What religion are you?"

If we took the same camera into most churches, people would typically respond by what they do at church: they tithe, they work in the nursery, and they read their Bibles and pray. In other words, we generally describe 'faith' by what we do religiously. In a very broad sense, faith is understood to be the flavor of religion we practice. So we hold inter-faith conferences and prayer meetings and intra-faith gatherings. As we toss this word around it fades and dilutes from its Biblical power. Faith becomes so much less than its original meaning.

What does the Bible say? Hebrews 11:1 from *The Message* says, *"The fundamental fact of existence is that this trust in God, this faith, is the firm foundation under everything that makes life worth living. It's our handle on what we can't see."* Faith is our gravity. Faith is what keeps our feet firmly grounded in the abundant life.

You know the beautiful moment in a wedding when the minister asks the couple to repeat the vows? They promise to be faithful to one another "until death do us part." When the Bible talks about faith, the word literally means "fidelity." Our faith is an expression of our faithfulness to God. When we choose doubt and self-service over faith and obedience, God considers that to be cheating on Him.

The Bible is clear that nothing happens in our relationship with God without faith. He does not operate outside of His covenant with us. In the same way a wife expresses her faithfulness to her husband by keeping herself for him only, we express our faithfulness to God by keeping our hearts and our minds pointed to Him. We express to Him our dependence, our thankfulness, our needs, our wants, our joys, and our sorrows, all within the context of faith.

So faith is a big deal. We often talk about faith as though it has little power, but in reality faith is the most powerful word in the Christian language. God's faithfulness to us and our expressions of faithfulness back to Him are the essence of what it means to be a Christian.

What is faith, really?

We can't understand this concept of faith without exploring what the Bible has to say about it. Christian faith means nothing apart from the Bible. Hebrews 11:6 from *The Message* states, *"It's impossible to please God apart from faith. And why? Because anyone who wants to approach God must believe both that he exists and that he cares enough to respond to those who seek him."*

Our first step, then, is to believe that God exists, that He is. Moses first encountered God on Mt. Sinai in the form of a burning bush. As God spoke to Moses, Moses wanted a name to call Him. Exodus 3:14 states, *"God said to Moses, 'I AM WHO I AM;' and He said, 'Thus you shall say to the sons of Israel, "I AM has sent me to you."'"*

Faith first requires that we acknowledge God as the I Am. We are not turning to our abilities, our spouses, our government, or our money to help us. We are depending on I Am. So, Biblically speaking, to worship Buddha is not faith because faith is only ascribed to I Am. Placing our faith in any other being or object is adultery and idolatry against I Am. God says He is a jealous God who wants all our affection and trust. He is a consuming God. He longs for us to point to Him with our whole hearts, our deepest affections. We must first believe that He is.

Jesus talked a lot about who He is. In John 6, the crowds asked Him for a sign so they would know how to believe Him. They reminded Jesus about how God provided them manna from heaven to sustain them and they asked Jesus for bread from heaven. Jesus responded by saying, "I Am the bread of life." He is the Source.

Jesus tells a story in John 10 about how a shepherd gets to his sheep. A shepherd does not go over the fence. Those who try to break in to the fold that way are thieves and robbers. The shepherd goes through the door and calls to his sheep and they follow him to green pastures. In this story, the abundant life is the green grassy field. We are the sheep. Jesus says, "I Am the door of the sheep." He is the only way to the abundant life.

In John 11, Jesus' friend Lazarus has died. Martha, his sister, is deeply grieved. Jesus tells her that Lazarus will rise again. "I know that he will rise again in the resurrection on the last day," she responds. Jesus says, "I Am the resurrection and the life." He is the One who can make dead things live again.

During His last moments on earth, the disciples ask Jesus, in John 14, to show them the way to the Father. Jesus responds, "I Am the way, the truth, and the life." He is the path to the Father.

In John 15 Jesus says, "I Am the vine." We are the branches. He is the nourishment for the branch to produce fruit.

In other Gospels, Jesus calls Himself the Light of the World, the Good Shepherd, and the Temple. The Book of Hebrews calls His body the "veil of the temple" and when His body was ripped, so was the veil that kept us from the Holy of Holies, the very presence of God.

So what do we take from this? What does this mean for daily life? When I need peace, I do not just need the attribute of peace. I need the Prince of Peace. When I need forgiveness, I need the Lamb of God who takes away my sins. When I am rejected and suffering, I need the God who *is* love. I need Jesus the Messiah, who in John 8 boldly declares that, *"before Abram was born, I Am!"*

God does not always answer our prayers with the outcome that we desire. But He **always** answers our prayers with Himself. Jesus says that when we are abiding in Him, He will always answer us. He will always show up personally as the Great I AM. If we ask Him for a fish, He will not give us a stone. If we ask Him for an egg, He will not give us a scorpion. He will always give us the Holy Spirit when we ask for anything (see Luke 11:11-13). When you ask Him for your deepest desires, you may not get your specific outcome, but you will always get Him. He will always be our Source. He is our I Am.

Secondly, faith requires that we believe in God's goodness. To understand this we have to go back to the very beginning of the Story. Remember the amazing and lavish garden God created for Adam and Eve? Remember the intimacy they shared? Remember how, after each day of creation, God declared His work good? Satan's deception aimed to discredit God's goodness. The crown of God's creation, the image-bearing children of His heart, rejected His goodness for their own independent purposes.

We, like them, reject God's goodness in order to quickly gain what we think we want. When we do not trust Him it is not because He lacks trustworthiness. We don't trust because we believe the same lie as Eve did: God is holding out on us, and we have to take what we want or He won't give it to us. Abiding in God turns quickly to striving for good, the "good" we want now.

In Deuteronomy 11, God told His people that if they loved Him with all their hearts and obeyed His commands, He would provide rain for their harvests. If they did not look to Him as their Source, the rain would stop. He was asking for their faith. As they moved into the Promised Land, the Israelites believed God (Yahweh) was the God of the "big stuff" like rescue from Egypt and conquering enemies. The everyday stuff, however, was less obvious and so Baal worship entered the scene. During the time of Elijah, the people of Israel had a terrible habit of worshipping Baal, a pagan god of rain and harvest, trusting their own ability to please a false deity rather than obeying the God of their fathers. When Elijah prayed for God to stop the rain, he was asking God to follow through with what was already stated: that if they turn and worship other gods, then Yahweh would *shut up the heavens so that there would be no rain*" (Deuteronomy 11:17). God labeled their lack of faith as idolatry and adultery against Him.

I don't worship Baal, but I do tend to rely on my own abilities to survive. I don't pray to anyone but God, but I sometimes act as if I can wield His power in my own life. In a sense, I count on God for the big stuff (like salvation) but my own striving is supposed to take care of the rest. God is not obligated to save us; He *wants* to save us. He is for us and came to give us abundant life. Baal and my own abilities eventually fail every time. God's goodness is the bedrock foundation of hope and trust.

Faith requires a trust in God's goodness as a starting point. So how do we build this kind of faith? How do we grow in this understanding and move from our heads to our hearts? Here are some ideas:

1.  We ask God to strengthen our heart faith in Him, like the man in Mark 9 who exclaimed to Jesus, "I believe. Help my unbelief!" Only God can strengthen us. We start by asking.

2.  We meditate on God's goodness as revealed in the life of Jesus and His word. Find the passages of the Bible that reveal God's amazing goodness and read them slowly, allowing them to soak in.

3.  We can remind ourselves of the truth of the Gospel. We need to pay close attention to what we have heard so we don't drift away from it. We need to find creative ways to keep the Good News fresh and not allow it to atrophy into a language that lessens its impact. Yes, Jesus died for our sins. But what does that mean to us now? How did that change things for you this morning? At work yesterday?

I am always fascinated by views about the hand of God from people trying to figure out the heart of God. His goodness is always put under the microscope when circumstances prove to be difficult, as if His goodness can only be proven if our circumstances are going well. If our difficult situation is not God's fault, then it must be our lack of goodness: did I do something to deserve this? But all our figuring and formulating about the correlation between God's goodness and ours reflects the heart of our fallen nature: we ate from the tree of the knowledge of good and evil and we think our goodness saves us and helps us avoid terrible tragedies and everyday struggles. We assume that if God is good enough then He would save us from bad circumstances. If we were good enough God would bless us with good circumstances. This contradicts the Bible and who God says He is. He binds broken hearts, assuming that our hearts are broken. The people of Hebrews 11 (the "faith chapter") were sometimes rewarded with good circumstances. Then, others of great faith *"were stoned, they were sawn in two, they were tempted, they were put to death with the sword."* The writer of Hebrews calls them, *"men of whom the world was not worthy."*

After the earthquake in Haiti in 2010, the Haitian believers were standing in the street singing "great is our God in all things" as bodies were pulled from wreckage. These people were those of whom the world is not worthy. My heart stands with them as a new courage rises in me to be loving but uncompromising in my faith. I have so much. Many of them were keeping severed limbs attached with duct tape. It is not the circumstances that prove or disprove God's goodness. It is the ability of God's people, in the midst of tragedy, standing with assurance that God's goodness is the bedrock of their hope, that proves His goodness.

When someone asks you about your faith, you can discuss where you go to church, or you can say you believe in Yahweh and you trust in His goodness.

WHAT IS OBEDIENCE?

For as long as I live on Earth, I will have a soul that lives in my body. When my body dies, my soul will have no earthly way to express itself. It's not that my body is more powerful or more important than my soul; I just have no other way, while I live on this planet, to express my soul than through my body. In the same way, we have faith that expresses itself through obedience. If we do not obey God through acts of our will, our faith has no expression; it is dead.

We don't just believe with our minds; we believe with our lives. Obedience is our expression of faith. If you are married, do you love your spouse with your mind or your life? Do you pledge fidelity but live as a single person? God is asking us to pledge our fidelity to Him and then act on that pledge, to point our whole beings toward Him. He doesn't want us just on Sundays. He does not need part-time Christians. Faith without obedience is dead.

Our surrender to His lordship is our obedience. *Obedience is how we surrender.* It is the practical, in the now, not-just-a-theory kind of surrender. It is not a feeling. In fact, obedience often goes against how we feel. Obedience is actually what God often uses to heal our feelings.

Obedience is knowing God's Word and applying it. We surrender our individual stories for His epic Story. And so, obedience has two steps: 1. Know God's Word, and 2. Apply it. That's it. Just do it. Why do we just do it? Because those who have gone before us have made it clear that obedience is the only thing that works. Obedience is the means by which we surrender and fear God. Surrender is what God uses to transform us. How does that work? I have no idea. I just know it does. When we surrender our lives to God, He does something that only He can do. And since He created us, He knows where we are broken and how to fix us. Obedience seems like a really good choice.

THE RESULT

God said, "Let there be light," and the solar system appeared. God said, "Heaven." The expanse appeared above the earth, and then He spoke the stars into existence. When God speaks, things happen. So when God makes promises, He keeps them … every time. When God says He will do something, He will. If God says it, it is written into the fabric of reality. We cannot base our faith on what our eyes see. We must base our fidelity and trust in God on what He has promised and His integrity to follow through on those promises. All His promises are 'yes' for us.

The danger is to believe that our faith produces God's results. We interpret faith wrongly when we assume the power of faith is ours to wield. Faith is not a striving work. Faith is an abiding trust. God uses His power in our behalf as a response to the volley of surrender as expressed through our faith and obedience.

In a culture that values personal safety and happiness above God's Story of radical adventure, we are often too afraid to allow His spiritual laws to rule our hearts. It is time to change that. Our heroes in Hebrews 11 changed the world forever. We are called to take the same faith to the next generation. We are called to live the abundant life with reckless abandonment.

God uses our acts of faith and obedience to further His Story. Sometimes the Storyline is advanced through victorious celebration. Lions are silenced. Fires are quenched. Wars are won. Prison doors fling open. Sight is restored. Heaven is brought to Earth.

Sometimes the Storyline is advanced through suffering. Pastors are tortured. Children are killed in front of their parents. Wives are raped in front of their husbands. Churches are burned. Privileges are denied. A Savior is crucified.

However God chooses to tell His Story, the ending is the same. Whatever happens to us, the characters in this epic Story, we will be there for the final bow. We will be raised and we will meet Him in the air. We will be like Him, and we will see Him face-to-face. There will be no more tears. No more fears. No more debts. No more pain. No more sin. No more death.

Sometimes God is asking us to walk in glorious victory. Sometimes we die humble and quiet deaths. Surrender is not for wimps.

Life requires certain natural laws to make it work. The abundant life requires certain spiritual laws to function. Faith and obedience are not about the outcome but about the process of surrender. If we want to move beyond sin management and works-driven Christianity, faith and obedience are the only options. We have been living outside of what God intended for so long that it seems normal. We need a new normal.

### Going Deeper

1. Before reading this chapter, how would you have answered someone who asked about your faith?
2. How would you answer now?
3. How has God proven His goodness to you? Give specific examples.
4. Jesus is the Bread, the Door, the Resurrection, the Way, the Truth, the Life, and the Vine. And that's just in the book of John. Who is the I Am for you?
5. Does obedience bring us to God, or come from a life with God, or both? Explain what you mean.
6. Are faith and obedience "normal" in your life?
7. How is your approach to your relationship with God different with this understanding?

# 8
# A New Normal:
## *Surrendering Everything*

*"God is only known through openness, surrender, and receptivity. He is not known through logic, analysis, or control." David G. Benner*

*"When the heart sees what God wants, the body must be willing to spend and be spent for that cause alone." Oswald Chambers*

*"There are two kinds of people: those who say to God, "Thy will be done," and those to whom God says, "All right, then, have it your way." C.S. Lewis*

I took a tennis class in college. After an entire semester I still don't understand how to keep score. I'm guessing some Englishman was completely intoxicated when he invented the scoring system. Love equals nothing. Confusing. Then we skip from 15 to 30 to 40? Very strange.

It was a warm afternoon in tennis class, as I was waiting for my opponent to begin her serve, when everyone in my class shouted, "LOOK OUT!" As I turned my head to see what was happening, a tennis ball nailed me in the face right between the eyes. I was thrown to the ground, glasses flying, and ended up with two black eyes. The girl who pegged me was three courts away, standing with a horrified look on her face, and all I could do was laugh (and cry a bit, too). I somehow passed tennis class and have never played again.

Sometimes we think this is how God plays with us. We ask Him to answer us, whatever the question might be, and we innocently wait for Him. Then a terrible situation comes out of nowhere, clocks us, and knocks us off our feet. *Lord, I asked for help and now it seems worse.* Sometimes it seems this game makes no sense at all, and we don't want to play anymore. We wonder how anyone is supposed to win or even what the score means. It often feels like God's love equals nothing.

But God doesn't play like that. And it takes faith to hit the ball back when we are not sure what He will send our way. God's goal is not to beat us in this game. His goal is to teach us to play with Him. He is not trying to score, unless it means to win our hearts. Because so much happens in our world outside the gravity-grounding principle of faith, unexpected events often float (or slam) onto the court. Like my tennis class, we are slammed in the face by something that did not come from God or us but from somewhere else. Something appears in our lives to own that neither of us put there. How does this work?

So how do we stay in a game that makes no sense to us? How do we stay engaged when isolation, addictions, entitlement, passivity, and independence seem so much safer and easier to manage? How does this look in real life?

## THE VOLLEY OF SURRENDER

As humans, we are powerful and weak, central and insignificant, eternal and mortal. We are powerful because we have the ability to make choices that influence the Storyline. We are weak because we cannot change anyone, even ourselves. We are central to God's Story of redemption, but we are insignificant, a tiny dot on the timeline in human history. We will live forever, but we are afraid to die.

There are so many things we cannot do. We cannot fly without assistance. We cannot simply stop an addiction. We can't make a husband change or a wife revert to how she used to be. As a culture, we say ridiculous things to cope with our inabilities. *God helps those who help themselves.* If we could help ourselves then we would not need a Savior to help us. *The only person you can change is yourself.* Really? Then why do I do the same things over and over again? We are powerful and yet weak.

The "game" works by really knowing Who has invited us to play. We need to know His heart and His love for us. Our first step in experiencing the abundant life is to engage in an authentic relationship with Jesus. He asks us to step onto the court and learn to volley with Him.

Often our Bible study teaches us much about Him, but does not help us to really know Him. Rather than read for information, read through one of the Gospels and insert yourself in the stories. Be the woman who, for twelve years, could not stop bleeding. Sit with the rejection and the pain of the constant reminder that you are "unclean." See Jesus walking through the crowd, and reach out and touch Him. See Him turn around to find you, point to you with compassion, and declare your healing … after twelve years. Have you struggled with anything for twelve years that needs His touch?

Or be another unclean person, a leper. Cry out to Jesus. As you tell Him that He could heal you if He is willing, hear Him say to you, "I am willing."

Be the blind Bartimaeus in Mark 10 and cry out to Jesus to have mercy on you. Let Him ask you what you want. Are you brave enough to tell Him? Can you own your desire with Him and risk His answer?

Everything that happens in the abundant life happens on the court of connection with God and others. Isolation and addictions deceive us and lead us to other kinds of survival life. But we cannot have this life without connecting to its Source. Get to know Him. Spend time connecting to His kindness and tenderness for you. Allow your faith to build as you meet Him as I AM and bask in His goodness. It is time to get in the game.

While connection is about oneness, ownership is about "otherness." In our relationship with God, oneness requires us to also be separate, to be autonomous. We do not lose our humanity when we connect with God. In fact, it is within our union with God that we become most fully human.

Therefore, pick up your ball and own what is yours. We can fully embrace all that is within us. While we cannot do much about what we own, we *can* claim it. We cannot own what belongs to others, but we can profess and confess what belongs to us. Ownership is the key to freedom. We own our design to point out and all the ways we have gone against that design. We own everything from our skin in, even if we have to own a stain on our hearts put there by someone else. If it is happening in us, it is ours.

God has given us many different human relationships to teach us how to connect with Him in healthy ways. The requirements for connection and separateness in healthy human relationships also apply to our relationship with God. The qualities of character that help or hurt our relationships with others do the same with our relationship with God. As we grow in relational health with God, we grow with others, and vice versa.

Where do you struggle in your relationships? What seems to always be your fault? What seems to always be the other's fault? What themes come up for you? What areas of your life seem impossible to surrender so you ignore them? How deep does your denial run? Mine is often Grand Canyon deep.

Can you be honest? "Normal" has always been rooted in our denial. It's time for a new normal, an exchange of all that we own for something else.

So we surrender. We cannot stop our sin, but we can confess it for healing. We cannot bind our broken hearts, but we can offer them to the One who can. We can't change our habits or hang-ups, but we can relinquish them to the Savior who can change us. We can breathe out what is ours and breathe in what God offers. We breathe out our sin and breathe in His forgiveness and cleansing. We breathe out our pain and breathe in His offered healing. God connects. God owns. And God surrenders what belongs to Him in exchange for what belongs to us.

In John 13, Jesus is washing the feet of His disciples. When He gets to Peter, a powerful conversation occurs. Peter feels uncomfortable allowing Jesus to serve him in this way. He stops Jesus and says, *"Never shall You wash my feet!"* A blatant refusal, Peter does not understand what is happening. Jesus replies, *"If I do not wash you, you have no part with Me."*

What does that mean?

I get what Peter is saying. Peter, after all, was the first to recognize that Jesus was the Messiah. Why would the Christ, the Son of God, wash his feet? Shouldn't it be the other way around? Isn't this Christian life about how we serve Jesus? Aren't we supposed to clean up our dirty feet so we can offer our Savior something good?

But Jesus was teaching Peter, and you and me, a truth that we must understand: Jesus must serve us. It is God's nature to point out of Himself. God is selfless and giving and does not do anything out of selfish ambition. It is like the sun trying to be dark. It cannot happen. God is love. To ask for our service without first serving us goes against His very grain. He always goes first.

But also, He must serve us to cleanse us from unrighteousness. We cannot do this for ourselves. We cannot save ourselves from our sins. We cannot make up the difference for the mistakes we have made. Only Jesus can bridge the gap. If we do not allow Him to serve us, we will miss the whole point. If we don't allow Jesus to offer His life in our behalf, we will miss salvation completely. He must wash our dirty feet to save us.

Peter finally understood. *"Lord, then wash not only my feet, but my hands and my head."* In the same way, we own the dirt on our feet and allow Jesus to wash not only our feet but our dirty hands and heads as well. Peter needed to change not only what he was thinking but also *how* he was thinking in order to receive all that Jesus had for him.

NEW THINKING

When I was about seven years old, I asked my parents for an Easter Bunny. I wanted a real bunny for Easter. They said no. When I was eight years old I asked my parents for a chimpanzee. I wanted my own pet monkey because I thought it would be the greatest thing ever. My parents said no. I begged. They said no. I cried. They still said no. I pulled the "you never give me what I want" fit, and they continued to say no. When I was nine years old I tried for a duck. I got a dog instead.

Sometimes we need to rethink how we are thinking. When a line of thinking doesn't work, we have to be willing to adopt a new one. Sometimes we don't get what we want from God because He knows something we cannot see. It is not that we didn't ask with faith or that we have been disobedient.

Surrender requires the maturity to allow God to know more than we do. God is in charge of the outcome, whatever it is. God never says we won't suffer. There is suffering in His Story. But God promises to walk with us, no matter what.

Transformation requires a willingness to surrender the old ways of thinking and learn how God thinks. This is hard because we don't always think about the need to think differently. A wise person once said that we can't solve a problem using the same thinking that caused the problem. When we renew our minds, our attitudes change. When we renew our minds, our feelings change. When we renew our minds, our behaviors change. Notice that God does not tell us to be transformed by the perfecting of our behaviors. The Christian life is not about 'sin management' but about heart renewal. This starts with the mind.

When we surrender our perspectives, attitudes, and thoughts to God, He renews them by His Spirit. When we are *trying* to live by faith, but our minds constantly doubt and rationalize, James tells us that we are 'double-minded' (see James 1:8). Purify your heart by surrendering it, again and again, to the One who can transform it. Things really can become new and different. We must renew our minds to find our new life. We must embrace our neediness to find abundance. We must lose our lives to find them.

## HUMBLE YOURSELF

Did you know that the New Testament talks about us 'in Christ' over 200 times? We don't surrender to God's commands for the sake of being 'good Christians.' We surrender to a person who can transform us in Christ.

Have you ever done something because you *had* to do it? Now compare that to when you have done the same thing because you *chose* to do it. What is the difference? There is something very different about doing the laundry because no one else will and doing it to serve someone. God wants us to want to surrender to Him. His first choice is that we humble ourselves, not for Him to humble us. As we willingly allow

Him access into our hearts and point to Him through our obedience and faith, we begin to walk with Him in a way that truly changes everything.

I met a man in Rwanda, a prison chaplain named Thomas who serves in a prison that houses some of the perpetrators from the genocide of 1994. Many of the prison chaplains in Rwanda serve some of the very people who murdered members of their own families. These men and women are the truest kind of heroes.

Thomas told a story of when he was a cattle farmer. His family owned many cows and felt blessed by God to be so fortunate. One particular year they had many calves. But soon after some of the calves were born, they were slaughtered in the night. Thomas knew the killer was a witch doctor that lived in his village, so he approached this man to confront him. Denying the charges, the witch doctor reported Thomas to the authorities for falsely accusing him (a crime in his country). Thomas was asked to appear before a judge at the end of the week, so he fled to the woods to pray for three days. Repeatedly, Thomas cried out to God for justice and defense. He asked God to make this all go away. He owned his fear and offered it to the Lord. He owned his anger and offered it to the Lord. Finally, Thomas said that he offered the outcome, whatever it may be, to the Lord.

He came out of the woods on the third day, prepared for anything to happen, to a large crowd gathering near his fields. People began to call to him, telling him to come quickly to see. There, in the middle of the field, stood the witch doctor, completely naked, with his arm stuck inside the cow's womb. Unable to remove his arm, the witch doctor was forced to follow the cow around all night long until he was discovered that morning. The witch doctor had been trying to harm another cow before it could be born. God vindicated Thomas as the whole village saw the witch doctor's guilt. Thomas humbled himself and pointed to God. God took care of the rest.

Can you trust God with the outcome? Can you choose a one-down position with God, allowing Him to orchestrate and weave together the outcome of His choosing? Can I? Are we willing to wrestle, like Thomas, until we have given all the consequences to our Savior? Some things require three days to work through. Some things require twelve years. No matter how long, God is asking us to wrestle through ourselves until we find the place of willing humility. God does not want token respect, but sincere humbleness. When surrender looks like this, there is no limit to what He will do in response.

## JESUS' EXAMPLE

Have you ever carried a suitcase too long? When you try to put it down your fingers burn from fatigue, and it is hard to straighten them? Sometimes our souls experience that same kind of exhaustion. We carry around our baggage (mine is bigger than carry-on), and it eventually becomes too much. It is hard to continue carrying it, but it is also hard to put down. We become afraid that if we drop any part of it we will be considered irresponsible, or worse, as the first pieces slip out of our tired hands we will drop it all. We need a way to release our stuff, whatever we need to own, and give it to someone stronger.

Our sense of independence creates a striving to be dependable, a person God can use. We cry out to Him for His strength and wisdom so we can do a better job for Him. Believing He is looking for autonomy and rule following, we endeavor to work hard to give up our many coping strategies. We stop smoking and drinking. What would Jesus do? He wouldn't smoke or drink, right? Wait, He did drink at a party, but He didn't get drunk. So I won't get drunk. But Jesus also never wore pants and probably never ate chocolate.

Instead of trying to understand *what* Jesus would or would not do, let's understand *how* He would have done it. Here's what sets Jesus apart: He never did anything outside of His oneness relationship with the Father. Ever. There are one hundred verses (literally) in the Book of John mentioning that Jesus only said and did what the Father told Him or showed Him. If Jesus did not live a God-honoring life His own way, then how am I supposed to do it? How are you? If Jesus, who is God, did not act independently of the Father, then how are we to live the Christian life apart from Him?

We read also, that Jesus often went to solitary places to pray. He needed to know what the Father was saying and doing. How else could He end up in the garden of Gethsemane and surrender His will?

When Jesus died on that cross, He was not thinking about you and me. He was thinking about His Father. The Father was thinking about you and me. The Father loved the world so much that He gave His only Son. The Son pointed to the Father. The Father pointed to us. Now we can point to Him. As a result, the Father points to the Son, and the Son points to us as His bride, and we can point to Him.

What would Jesus do? He would surrender. How would Jesus do it? With deep humility, placing His Father and us before Himself. He was perfect.

While speaking to a friend about her constant struggle with perfectionism, I asked her what she thought she would be able to do if she was perfect that she can't do now? She responded, "I could stop the same sins that I keep doing over and over again. I would be stronger." I often think this way and I don't think I am alone.

But is perfection really about strength? Is perfection about our ability to overcome and rightly behave? Hmmm...

When Jesus was in the garden of Gethsemane, He cried out to the Father to take such a terrible cup from Him. He was so grieved and distressed that He began to sweat blood.

Crying out to God, expressing His frustration with His disciples, and experiencing anguish as He faced the most important moments of His earthly life, Jesus was far from a picture of strength and ability. He was in the turmoil of blood, sweat, and tears (literally) and yet He always came back to complete surrender to the Father. Three times, He begged His Abba to spare Him the cross. Three times, He surrendered His will. It was His surrender, not His lack of struggle, that made Him perfect. It was His willingness to be weak that marked His perfection.

I tend to think, intuitively, that perfection means I am independently strong. But Jesus, fully human, and our example of what it looks like to be created in God's image, was perfect because He was humble. Perfection is not our ability to overcome. Perfection is our ability to surrender. We must be willing to walk the path toward perfection, not by our striving efforts, but by our constant willingness to allow God to lead. Jesus, the Son of Man, did just that. He was perfect.

This is the perfection God is calling us to embrace. He is asking us to surrender what we own within the context of our intimate relationship with Him. That's it. That is the abundant life. That is the art of breathing. We are asked to constantly, consistently wrestle through ourselves, with stark honesty, even with bloody sweat, to get to our own end and surrender the outcome to Jesus. He is not asking us to do anything that He has not already willingly done.

## SURRENDER PRAYER

Sometimes we don't know how to express this humility. The disciples asked Jesus how they should pray, and He taught them what we call the Lord's Prayer. The following prayer is based on the outline and progression of thought of that prayer. It is not meant to be a replacement for or repetition of that prayer, but instead its purpose is to assist us in how we can pray and wrestle through ourselves to come to a place of surrender. It is an example of what surrender can look like. Quiet your heart and read slowly:

*Lord God, I first come and worship who You are. You are the source of my life. You are the breath that I breathe. You are the one who makes breathing possible. You created everything that is ... with words. Your power is unmatched in both the Heavenly realms and here on earth. You are the author of my Story. And it is Your Story that I have been invited into. Lord, I often lose sight of that. But today, I surrender my story to yours.*

*There is no way I can make my story work together for my good. You know I've tried. It is not in me. But in Your Story there is nothing impossible. In Your Story, the happy ending is guaranteed. I have my version of what a happy ending looks like. But I need to surrender it to Your Story. You may have a completely different picture. This scares me. I own my fear and offer it to You now. I'm scared of what will happen to me if You don't answer in the way I'm picturing. I need Your peace. I need Your guidance. I need Your outcome, no matter what my picture is because Your Story is always leading me to my best. My story is always leading me to my momentary happiness. I choose to trust You.*

*I choose to trust that You know more than I do. I choose to trust that You are good ... no matter what happens. Jesus offered His desire to You, but willingly surrendered it to Your plan. Your Word says that it was for the joy set before Him that He endured that cross. I own my confusion about my situation. I own my fear. I own my pain. I own my stuck feelings. I own my anger with You for not moving in the way I want You to. I surrender these things to You and ask that, no matter how I FEEL, Your will would be done. Because somewhere I know that the joy on the other side will make this endurance worth it.*

*So please give me my daily bread to sustain me as I take baby steps forward into Your will for my life. I'm asking for wisdom because I need it, and You ALWAYS say yes to that. I trust You with my heart, even if I can't understand what Your hands are doing. When the waves of shame or fear or anger hit me, I ask that You would provide exactly what I need for those moments. I'm not asking to feel good all the time, although I would really like that. I understand, however, that I just need my daily bread. I will let tomorrow worry about itself, and I will focus on Your goodness today. You always help me in the now.*

*I confess my entitlement, my shame, my addictions, my passive anger, and my need to control. I confess my words, my actions, my thoughts, my attitudes, and my feelings that have not aligned with Your Story and what You have asked of me. I offer them to You for healing. And Father, as I offer these things to You, I also stand before You and offer my forgiveness to those who have hurt me. I surrender the pain, the anger, and my need for justice to You and ask that You would guide me in what needs to happen next. I want to look like You and experience Your freedom with others.*

*So Father, guide me. Lead me back into Your Story today. I know that suffering will come, but You will walk through it with me. I'm counting on You to be who You say You are. I will take You at Your Word. I love You, and I trust You. In Jesus' name, Amen.*

## Going Deeper

1. Read Mark 10:46-52. Place yourself in the position of Bartimaeus. Experience his blindness that keeps him from what he wants. What is keeping you from what you want? Now imagine the crowds pull you up to Jesus. He asks, "What do you want?" How do you respond?

2. How deep is your denial about what belongs to you? What is "normal" in your life that sabotages abundance for you?
3. Have you ever allowed Jesus to "wash your feet" or are you trying to "clean yourself up" for Him?
4. Are you tired of "sin management" yet?
5. Like my friend, Thomas, is there an outcome you need to surrender to God?
6. If perfection is about weakness and surrender instead of independent strength, how does this change things?
7. After reading the Surrender Prayer, what does surrender feel like?

# 9

# How We Heal:
## *Surrendering the Wounds*

*"God is so vastly wonderful, so utterly and
completely delightful, that he can, without anything
other than himself, meet and overflow the deepest
demands of our total nature, mysterious and deep
as that nature is." A.W. Tozer*

*"Surrender is the foundational dynamic of
Christian spirituality—surrender of my efforts to
live my life outside the grasp of God's love and
surrender to God's will and gracious Spirit who
now becomes an abiding inner presence."
David G. Benner*

*"Life is not a problem to be solved; it is an adven-
ture to be lived." John Eldredge*

The New Testament Greek word for "to save" can also
be translated "to heal." In other words, as Christians,
when we talk about being saved, we are not just expressing
how we have been snatched from Hell. This idea of salvation includes an often overlooked but incredibly powerful

principle: God wants to heal us from the fall. He wants to make us new.

So how does this healing process look? The answer lies in how everything heals and grows. If I cut my leg open, it is true that I need some kind of knowledge to be able to begin the process of restoration. But that knowledge does not do the healing work. My head does not inform my leg what is required for healing. My head informs me to action, and it is the action that sets the stage for the healing of my leg. And there is something built-in to my leg that draws it, in the right environment, to healing. The actual re-sewing of my leg, however, is mysterious and even sacred. Healing is a miracle.

In the case of the fallen human heart, the healing process is much the same. Our heads cannot simply inform our broken hearts to mend. And yet, much of what we do at church, in our small group Bible studies, and our own personal quiet-times are just that. With enough information, we are taught, our hearts are just supposed to heal.

But they don't. We keep sinning. We keep isolating, practicing addictions, feeling entitled, passively waiting for our lives to change and when they don't we do things our own independent ways. We need some knowledge of how to start, and what the process looks like, so we can engage rather than inform our hearts. Within our fallen human hearts God created something that draws us to His healing. We just need to set the right environment.

WHAT WE NEED TO KNOW

To start, we must clearly define the wound. Because everything that happens in the abundant life happens through relationship, and the fall was a fall from our relationship with God, our healing can only come through relationship. Behavior change will not solve it. While there are behaviors that set the stage for healing, they do not cause it. Healing is a mystery.

When mankind's relationship with God was ripped apart, God spoke to Adam and Eve. As we read in Genesis 3:16-17, it is easy to hear anger in God's voice.

> *To the woman He said, "I will greatly multiply Your pain in childbirth, In pain you will bring forth children; Yet your desire will be for your husband, And he will rule over you. Then to Adam He said, "Because you have listened to the voice of your wife, and have eaten from the tree about which I commanded you, saying, 'You shall not eat from it'; Cursed is the ground because of you; In toil you will eat of it All the days of your life.*

For a moment, replay this passage but substitute a lamenting voice for an angry voice. Hear the pain and sorrow from a Creator to His Creation as He addresses their sin and their fate. Hear the hurt and betrayal in His voice.

He knew something that we need to understand. When we, like Eve, look to human relationships to fill the deepest parts of our souls, we feel controlled. Our wound is not that we have low self-esteem and cannot seem to connect with others the way we know we should. Our wound is that we have been cut off from the Source of relationships and now all our relationships leave us feeling rejected and controlled.

God names Adam's wound as well. Without God as the Source, nothing works according to its design. When we, as Adam's children, look to accomplishments to define and support us, we will experience a sense of failure. We will never be enough.

Don't we see this every day? Women looking for spouses and friends and children to address the longing for intimate connection in their hearts, only to feel rejected and controlled by them. Women experience deep rejection and fear being alone above everything else.

When Adam turns to his work as his source, he experiences failure. Men try to climb the corporate ladder, achieve the top sales, and win at every kind of competition imaginable, even if they have to invent the contest. Above every other fear in a man's heart is the fear of failure. He doesn't want to be found lacking.

We have all the same needs now as we did before the fall, but we lost our Source for meeting those needs. It is like finding ourselves alone on a tiny island surrounded by an ocean of salt water with only one tiny pond in the middle. The water in this little pond, however, is tainted. Every time we drink it, we become sick. What do we do? We drink the water. Why? What choice do we have if we want to survive? In this same way, we cope with being disconnected by sinning. How?

Everything we do outside of faith is sin. Everything. But what choice do we really have? If we are truly our only source for survival, and everything we do outside of a oneness connection with God is sin, we are in bondage to sin. Without God as our Source, we are left to figure out what is right for us individually. The last verse in the Book of Judges sums our situation up beautifully, *"Everyone did what was right in his own eyes."*

We are stuck in a world where truth is relative, and right and wrong are defined by personal preference, selfishness, and greed. Women seek relationships to fill the God-invented needs. Rather than experiencing fulfillment, they are left feeling controlled and rejected. Men strive to overcome and beat failure by being the best, constantly worried they are not really enough and do not actually have what it takes. Looking for success to quench the divinely designed needs, they are plagued by failure and shame. This is the curse. This is the problem that haunts us all.

Often we go to church to try and fix this. We put on our Sunday school faces and show up with smiles to receive our instruction on how *not* to do what others are *not* doing so we can fit in. We try to be "good Christians." We settle into our inability to be perfect and excuse our lack of faith on our humanness. And so we live as unhealthy people. We live as those who are unhealed.

## FEELINGS

Our desire for healing most often originates from feelings of pain. While feelings do not always tell us the truth, feelings always reveal our beliefs. Our beliefs reveal the lies that drive us. In other words, our feelings inform us of where we are, but not necessarily where we need to go. They make a terrible compass. Feelings are not facts; they are signals telling us what we actually believe.

If a tiny spider walks into my room, and I completely freak out, my feelings inform me of what I really believe about the spider. My degree of fear indicates my intensity of belief. If a seven-foot tarantula walks into my room, and I completely freak out, my feelings are more accurately aligned with truth. As I own my feelings, I discover more and more about what I believe and am able to evaluate where I am and where I need to head. If I do not own my feelings, they will often own me. I will feel driven by my emotions and unable to see the big picture.

The purpose of my feelings, in the transformation process, is not to guide me to where I want to go, but rather inform me about where I have been and what I have learned along the way. For example, if significant people have abandoned me in my life, it becomes easy to allow the fear of abandonment to drive my relationships. With my feelings in the driver's seat, each significant relationship in my life will be threatened by the past relationships. In a fallen world, our feelings do not lead us to what we have. In our brokenness, our feelings lead us to what we lack. They give us insight but not necessarily guidance.

Now that we are all flayed and exhausted, we need some good news. We need a new way of seeing our old ways of living. For some, the conversion experience was like the apostle Paul's in its intensity and transformation, encountering God in a miraculous way. For others, coming to Christ was a gradual process and, while there were definite markers along the way, the change was slow. However we have come to Christ, He is inviting us deeper still. But we must be honest about our independent approach to our sanctification. We could not save ourselves, and we cannot sanctify ourselves either.

In order to grasp this, we must start in God's Story. Here we must give up our right to be happy and allow God to address our deep need to be holy. As Americans, we value the pursuit of happiness. But when that cultural value is imposed on how our Creator is working in us, we miss Him. We say things like, "God would want me to be happy, right? If I'm not happy in my marriage then I should try to find someone who makes me happy." We truly believe God's first priority, as a loving parent, would be our happiness. But happiness depends on what is happening. We are asking God to control things, arrange our circumstances, so that we will be satisfied. But God knows we need to be holy. Holiness and wholeness are the same thing. To be holy and to be whole (or healed completely) are identical. If we are whole, are we not completely set apart from a broken world?

Coping is not healing nor is it a conscience thing. But within our safe relationship with God, and as others are included, we have the ability to honestly name what we are doing. We can openly name the ways we deal with feeling rejected and controlled. We can honestly deal with our failures. We start by being completely honest in the safety of connection. And then we hit the end of ourselves.

## THE ROMANS 7 WALL

As we are honest about our feelings and truly own them, we will come to the conclusion that we cannot fix what is wrong. We can't stop feeling these things. We cannot just stop protecting ourselves.

I have completed two marathons. Training experts make it clear that there will come a point during the race when each runner will feel an inability to continue. The body will hit "the wall" and the brain will side with the body to stop. This wall is so challenging, and so normal, that it forces trainers to address it clearly, so their runners do not give up in hopelessness.

The "Romans 7 Wall" has sidelined many trying to run the race of faith. And so it would be a great injustice for God not to warn us that coming to the end of our abilities is a necessary part of the process. We come to a place where we truly cannot change anything about ourselves. Paul experienced this as well. He wrestled through his own issues and, in Romans 7:18-24 (from *The Message*), came to this conclusion:

> *I realize that I don't have what it takes. I can will it, but I can't do it. I decide to do good, but I don't really do it; I decide not to do bad, but then I do it anyway. My decisions, such as they are, don't result in actions. Something has gone wrong deep within me and gets the better of me every time. It happens so regularly that it's predictable. The moment I decide to do good, sin is there to trip me up.*

Can you relate to this? The things we want to do, we don't do. The things we don't want to do are the very things we do. Argh. And so, we fall into our "sin management" rut and try to produce the "right fruit" and keep up the appearance. We try and try but fail again and again.

We cannot heal ourselves. We were never meant to. When we encounter the Truth, but our feelings and experience do not match, we must remain in that place of "stuck" rather than try to immediately solve it. We need to expect the Wall.

This is so hard. We live in a world that values efficiency. Those who solve problems quickly are considered healthy, while those who feel stuck seek counseling. We don't like feeling stuck. We pick the shortest lines at the bank, and the fastest route to our destination even if it is a longer distance. We want to keep moving. We feel enraged by a traffic light that skips us in its cycle. We are frustrated by the incompetence of every other driver on the road. We do not like intersections that make us stop, so we yield instead.

When God's Truth and our feelings intersect, both trying to lead us in opposite directions, we must persevere in this place for a moment. We must stop. We must hit the wall instead of trying to overcome it. We were not made to conquer it. God built this wall to bring us to the end of our own road. While our feelings help us understand where we have been and what we have learned, embedded into our experiences are lies that feel true. Our feelings are often testifying to lies, not to the Truth. The *facts* of our encounters have actually drawn us away from the *Truth*, and we are left feeling restless to feel better. We must stop, remain, and persevere in this place so that God can heal the feelings with His Truth. We must be willing to hit the wall and find the end of ourselves there.

THE GREAT EXCHANGE

The sting of death is sin. Often, our suffering is so subtle we do not know we are actually in pain. In a letter to the Church in Laodicea, John writes the following in Revelation 3:15-20:

*I know your deeds, that you are neither cold nor hot;
I wish that you were cold or hot. So because you are
lukewarm, and neither hot nor cold, I will spit you out
of My mouth. Because you say, "I am rich, and have
become wealthy, and have need of nothing," and you
do not know that you are wretched and miserable
and poor and blind and naked, I advise you to buy
from Me gold refined by fire so that you may become
rich, and white garments so that you may clothe
yourself, and that the shame of your nakedness will
not be revealed; and eye salve to anoint your eyes so
that you may see. Those whom I love, I reprove and
discipline; therefore be zealous and repent. Behold,
I stand at the door and knock; if anyone hears My
voice and opens the door, I will come in to him and
will dine with him, and he with Me.*

We often use the last verse in this passage for the purpose of evangelism, stating that Jesus is standing at the door
of your heart and wants to come in and have fellowship with
you. While this is a powerful image, the context of this verse
is actually for Christ-followers who have forgotten who their
Source really is.

The American church reflects the conditions of the
church of Laodicea. We acquire wealth and think we do not
need anything. Worse, we believe our wealth is God's stamp
of approval on us. We interpret our abundance of resources
as the abundant life. Not only are we privileged to drive a
car; we drive nice cars and live in lush homes with big yards
and swimming pools. There is nothing wrong with stuff. But
when our accumulation of stuff is carried out to its logical
end, we believe that God blesses us more than any other
nation. We must be some kind of "special" Christians who
have the ability to draw God's favor by working hard. We,
as a whole, have grown independent of our Source. We have

stopped needing Him; we just want His stuff. Without our desperation for God, however, we have become lukewarm. Jesus states that He wants to (literally) vomit His lukewarm followers out of His mouth. Our self-sufficiency makes Him sick.

We think we are rich. God says we are wretched, pitiful, poor, blind, and naked. We have thoughts that are not from God, our Source. We say words that do not reflect God, our Source. We participate in acts of vengeance (often very subtly) and seek our own ways. We justify, deny, and cover up our sin and think we do not need anything because we can pay our bills. We tithe, volunteer, and work hard, but we do not forgive a father for being distant in childhood or a sibling for saying mean things ten years ago. We think we are fine as the source for our own lives. We are managing our sin well, or so we think. We are coping well and surviving the fall, but missing the abundant life altogether.

Our gold will not make us rich, but Jesus' will. Our robes do not cover our pitiful nakedness. His do. Our blindness is not corrected by our striving because we cannot bear what we see in ourselves when we really look. But His salve will heal our eyes. Matthew 5:3 tells us, *"Blessed are the <u>poor in spirit</u>, for theirs is the kingdom of heaven."* We need to admit we are poor and buy from Jesus, our Source. In our poverty, we are rich. In God's Story, our stories start to make sense.

We are supposed to hit the "Romans 7 Wall," that place where we realize we cannot change ourselves. We are supposed to feel the reality of our bondage to sin. But Jesus came to bind broken hearts and set captives free. This was His mission from the beginning of the Story. He came to save us.

If you feel trapped in your past, you are at the right spot for healing. If you realize you are wretched, pitiful, poor, blind, and naked, you are exactly where you need to be. You are all those things. So am I. But God does not leave us there. Let's read Romans 8:1-3:

> *Therefore there is now no condemnation for those who are in Christ Jesus. For the law of the Spirit of life in Christ Jesus has set you free from the law of sin and of death. For what the Law could not do, weak as it was through the flesh, God did: sending His own Son in the likeness of sinful flesh and as an offering for sin, He condemned sin in the flesh.*

What we could not do, God did. In the same way we trust Him for our eternal outcome, we trust Him to heal us now. As we own our thoughts, motives, perspectives, and feelings, we can exchange them for His thoughts, motives, perspectives, and feelings. While it is not always instantaneous, it is always offered. God, through Jesus, is offering to be our Source in every way. What we could not do, He has already done for us.

## JESUS IS THE VINE

When we abide in Christ, as our Source, He makes Himself responsible for the fruit in our lives. When we have surrendered that unyielding feeling or behavior to Him, Jesus takes personal responsibility for fixing it. He replaces the old fruit with new. This fruit, the fruit of the Spirit, replaces the lust, the drive for happiness, the pleasure seeking, and all that we use to replace the true fruit He desires for us. We don't try to produce the fruit of the Spirit; we abide in Christ so He can do it.

How does He do this? The life-giving sap that runs through the vine to the branches is His grace. Where sin increases grace abounds.

Grace is not just bigger than sin; it is fundamentally different from sin. Sin is imparted through the Law, through all the "do's and don'ts." Grace is imparted through faith. Sounds like a lot of Christianese again, doesn't it? So let's say it like this: Grace is a *power*, given by God, through faith in Jesus, which enables us to overcome sin and be transformed. The Law points out our sin. Grace overcomes our sin. What the Law could not do, Christ did.

When we think about the Law, as Americans living in this era, we feel a bit disconnected from the First Century Jewish understanding of the word. For us, the implication would be equivalent to all the formulas and efforts we do to be "good Christians" and thus win God's favor. We all do this. But the abundant life is not about behavior change. We need transformational heart change.

The apostle Paul, a former persecutor of Christians, testified again and again that it was grace that gave him the ability to change. Paul understood that he was a changed man because grace was the power behind his labor to change … and it worked. God's grace did not prove vain. When we seek to be justified or righteous without grace we are missing the point.

Paul also tells us that when we seek to justify ourselves by what we do, we have fallen from grace. If we are seeking to be justified before God by being good, doing all the right things, and judging others who do not live up to that, we are headed down the wrong path. If we seek to humbly accept what Jesus has done for us and truly receive His gift, we will walk down the path of grace that leads to the abundant life. The path is that of surrender. We must surrender to the Source to receive His grace.

God's grace is the best news of all. It is the power to save, build up, sanctify, and justify. The sap of God's grace flowing though our lives causes obedience through faith, abundance, contentment and sufficiency, and the ability to approach the very throne of God. It points us away from the shackles of always getting it right to the freedom of learning to fly.

Grace is not based on our merit, but on God's unchanging, unflinching, always perfect, always generous character. We heal through abiding. We abide through surrender.

## Going Deeper

1. Eve's curse left her feeling controlled and rejected in relationships. Can you relate to this when you look to people as your source of relational needs?
2. Adam's curse focused on his sense of failure. What happens in your relationship with God when you fail?
3. Do your feelings determine your decisions? Do you find yourself often acting against what you know because your feelings are so strong?
4. What priority, if you are completely honest, do you place on your happiness?
5. What does the "Romans 7 Wall" feel like to you? Do you see it as an obstacle or an opportunity?
6. In what ways are you "poor in spirit?"
7. If Jesus is responsible for the fruit in your life, what is your role?

# Living...

- existing; active; alive; breathing

*"Our soul is restless until it finds rest in Thee, O Lord."* St. Augustine

*"Go confidently in the direction of your dreams. Live the life you've imagined."* Thoreau

*"Don't live the length of your life, live the width of it as well."* Diane Ackerman

*"But life is no longer boring, resentful, depressing, or lonely because we have come to know that everything that happens is part of our way to the house of the Father."* Henri Nouwen

*"I dwell in possibility."* Emily Dickenson

The abundant life is not for wimps. We do not get this life without dying to ourselves and all the ways we are trying to survive apart from God. And as we die to live, we discover something else: we were never made to live for ourselves. Like a living cell in a body passes nutrients to the next cell, so we, in the body of Christ, live for the purpose of offering life to others. Instead of filling our buckets, we are asked to be the faucet and participate with God to save the world.

# 10
# Abiding:
## *Living in the Vine*

*"There is no graft without wounding—the laying
bare and opening up of the inner life of the tree
to receive the stranger branch. It is only through
wounding that access can be obtained to the fellowship of the sap and the growth and the life of the
stronger stem." Andrew Murray*

*"I am the true vine." Jesus*

*"The spiritual life does not remove us from the
world but leads us deeper into it." Henri Nouwen*

When Jesus called His disciples, He said, "Follow me."
But before His death and resurrection Jesus upgraded
His command to, "Abide in me." Jesus was asking them (and
us) to do more than just follow His example. He was calling
us to something much deeper than a *lifestyle* that reflects
God's goodness. He wants the most vulnerable, most pro-
tected parts of us. Instead of coping with and attempting to
manage our sin, He is asking that we surrender our wounds.
He knows the wounds are the fertile ground from which sin
will grow.

He is asking us to abide and heal in Him. But how?

When a gardener wants to engraft a branch into a vine, he must do several things. First, he must wound the vine. A selected place on the vine is torn open and exposed in order to receive the raw, cut branch. The branch is likewise cut from its original vine at an angle that matches the new vine's wounded opening. The branch is united with the vine, their wounded parts flush with each other, and the branch remains there. Over the process of healing, the vine and the branch heal and fuse together as one, allowing the life-giving sap of the vine to flow directly into the branch. As this process strengthens the branch, it begins to bear fruit. The gardener prunes the branch and tends to its health so it can bear even more fruit. Within this union of the branch and the vine, of vulnerable wounds touching and healing, a harvest comes.

*"I am the true vine, and My Father is the vinedresser. Every branch in Me that does not bear fruit, He takes away; and every branch that bears fruit, He prunes it so that it may bear more fruit. You are already clean because of the word which I have spoken to you. Abide in Me, and I in you. As the branch cannot bear fruit of itself unless it abides in the vine, so neither can you unless you abide in Me. I am the vine, you are the branches; he who abides in Me and I in him, he bears much fruit, for apart from Me you can do nothing. If anyone does not abide in Me, he is thrown away as a branch and dries up; and they gather them, and cast them into the fire and they are burned. If you abide in Me, and My words abide in you, ask whatever you wish, and it will be done for you. My Father is glorified by this, that you bear much fruit, and so prove to be My disciples" (John 15:1-8)*

Jesus is the Vine. The Gardener (the Father) was *"pleased to crush Him"* for us (Isaiah 53:10). Jesus was pierced for our transgressions. The Vine was wounded and exposed in order to receive us in a great union. By His wounds, we are healed. But we are healed *in* Him, not outside of a oneness relationship with the Vine.

We are the branches. We have been cut from our former lives of bondage to sin. Our testimonies show this clearly. Did you come to Christ because everything was going so well and, since you never experienced pain before, knew that God had prevented any and all suffering in your life? Jesus did not come for the healthy; He came for the sick. He is called a Savior because we need saving. Our old resources (isolation, addictions, entitlement, passivity, and independence) were not bringing lasting fruit. Painfully cut from our old ways, the angle of the cut fits exactly into the wound of the Vine.

Whatever you have been through, Jesus has a matching wound for you. Your wounds fit perfectly into His. He bore your sin in His body on the cross.

As we allow the intimate connection of our wounds with the wounds of Jesus, our raw places are no longer exposed. Jesus becomes our shield and protector. Our lives are truly hidden in Him. He understands our wounds at the deepest levels. As we stay there, remain, abide in that place, we are healed with the Vine in a mysterious union. We become one with the Vine. The sap of God's grace and fullness flows right into our spirits, filling us in a way that nothing else can. As the grace flows, the fruit grows. No striving is required for these amazing attributes to sprout out of what was once a dying branch. The fruit of the Spirit, God's very essence, flows right through us and out to a dying world. Jesus exchanges our old fruits (sins) for His fruit of the Spirit.

*Lust becomes Love.* Our need for intimacy and oneness was traded in for romance and lust when we become our own source. But when the Vine heals those disconnected places of lust, His fruit of love pours out of our lives. Agape love, the unconditional love of God, comes only through God's presence in us. It is the only water that can quench the love-starved soul and satisfy it.

*Happiness becomes Joy.* Happiness depends on what is happening. Happiness is a temporary, blissful experience that only lasts as long as conditions allow. When we mistake happiness for joy, we believe we cannot experience it in the marriage we are in, or the job we are doing, or with children who act like this, or because we are single. The demand for happiness is bondage to our circumstances. Joy is the actualization of our freedom and gives us strength in any circumstance, allowing us to live in the hope of what we do not yet see. Happiness requires a lot of work to arrange. Joy gives us the stamina to work anyway.

*Pleasure becomes Peace.* Peace is a contented restfulness within us that calms us and gives us strength. When peace is not produced in us, pleasure is a cheap, temporary imitation. Pleasure calms the chaos inside, but only briefly. Not all pleasure is bad. Not every distraction is wrong. But pleasure is not peace. Only Jesus can calm the human heart and bring true unity and lasting resolution to conflict, both inter-personally and intra-personally. True, Biblical peace is only obtained through the intimate connection with the Prince of Peace.

*Passivity becomes Patience.* We think that patience means we just have to wait. We tend to perceive it as a behavior, like sitting still in church and not skipping forward in line. But patience is so much more. A patient heart is able to compassionately endure another's faults and wait, sometimes years, for them to change. Patience is active and engaging, not passive and detached. We mistake God's patience for passivity and assume He has not acted because He won't make things change. But this is simply not true.

God is patient and produces the fruit of patience in our lives, giving us the ability to endure the way He does.

*Tolerance becomes Kindness.* Tolerance is the attitude that says, "I do my thing and you do yours, and we'll stay out of each other's way." Intolerance is often a terrible thing, but tolerance is not the fruit of the Spirit, kindness is. Kindness is a heart-felt reaching out; going out of our way to offer someone else what is needed. It reflects the heart of God being actively expressed through His people. It is God's kindness that leads us to repentance. It is the fruit of kindness that leads others to God's grace so that they may repent as well.

*Political Correctness becomes Goodness.* "Christian Culture," that Christian bubble we believers tend to find ourselves in, often defines what is Biblical by what we do not do, rather than what we actively do. Saying the right words and avoiding certain sins does not make a person good. When called "good," Jesus asked, *"Why do you call me good? There is only one who is good!"* (Matthew 19:17) Goodness comes from the Good One, God alone. Without Him, we have a watered-down, politically correct version of this fruit. With Him, we stand against the evil that seeks to destroy every good thing on this planet. Without God's goodness, there is nothing good.

*Independence becomes Faithfulness.* Faithfulness is fidelity to someone. It is a pointing out even when circumstances are difficult. Independence is an assertion of personal rights. Rather than remaining loyal, we tend to pull our freedom card and indulge our "rights" rather than doing the right things. We, as a culture, are not very good at faithfulness at all. But why should we be? Faithfulness is not simply a behavior, but a fruit of the Spirit. Faithfulness is the gravity that holds our feet to the abundant life.

*Greed becomes Gentleness.* The meek shall inherit the earth, but we try to take it by force. It is through gentleness that we gain, not greed. When I lived in New York, the driving motto was "take the road or it will be taken from you." We take the best parking places from people who need them while we sport Christian fish stickers on the back of our cars. We shame grocery store clerks for giving us the wrong change on our way to church. And then we assume God is the same way. We see His angry eyes when we have sinned and assume He will be harsh. But when God heals the entitled greed within us, His gentleness spills out of our lives to others.

*Blame becomes Self-Control.* Just like Adam and Eve, we look for someone to blame rather than take ownership and responsibility for ourselves. We blame to avoid feeling judged. Self-control is learned when we sin and are loved anyway. The healing experiences of God's grace cleansing the shame allows us to fully own and surrender rather than blame.

## ABIDING

Imagine a live sponge in the ocean. The sponge remains in the water, never becoming separate from it. The sponge is abiding in the water, but the water is also abiding in the sponge. While they are autonomous entities, they are also one. The sponge would die outside the water. The water fills every pore of the sponge, saturating it completely, keeping it alive. The sponge contains the water and, as a result, produces life-giving nutrients to the surrounding underwater life. Without sponges contributing to the ecosystem, it would be severely out of balance. So it is with us. We abide in Christ, and Christ abides in us. We would die without Him. But without our abiding, the world around us would die as well.

The word *abide*, in Strong's Dictionary, means this: "*to remain; to tarry; not to depart; to continue to be present; to be held, kept continually; not to become another.*" Sometimes this word is translated *endured.*

We must abide, persevere. We don't give up. We don't pull away. We remain. We stay. We resist what is evil and stand for what is good. As we do this, character is forged within us. This character, as we have seen, allows us to experience the profound hope of God's Story. Character opens the sap-lines within our branch-engrafted lives. Character is required for healthy fruit. Our suffering produces abiding perseverance, our perseverance character, and character hope. This hope is not for us alone but also for a dying world.

## GOD'S STORY AND MY STORY

The fruit is not for the sake of the branch. In fact, the branch does not personally benefit from the fruit itself. The branch benefits from the amazing, life-giving, nourishing sap flowing through it. We don't produce the fruit of the Spirit for ourselves.

In the same way the vine and the branches heal together to form an inseparable union, our individual stories become caught up in, and transcended by, God's Story of redemption. For some reason, God has chosen to produce the life-giving fruit through His people. God does not stop rulers from corruption. He does not stop the rapist from his crimes. God does not "make us" choose wisely or stop our voices from yelling at loved ones. God has chosen for His Story to play out through our stories, and this cannot happen unless He works through us. He is not changing the world through manipulation and control (devices of His enemy); God is changing the world through His people, through the fruit that springs forth from His branches. With Him and in Him, we become the tree of life. Revelation 22:1-2 says:

> *Then he showed me a river of the water of life, clear as crystal, coming from the throne of God and of the*

*Lamb, in the middle of its street. On either side of
the river was the tree of life, bearing twelve kinds of
fruit, yielding its fruit every month; and the leaves of
the tree were for the healing of the nations.*

God's plan to heal the nations is the fruit of this tree.
The fruit comes from the branches, you and me. There is no
other option. God did not create a "Plan B" if we fail to pro-
duce fruit. While the branch will die without the Vine, the
Vine has no fruit without the branches. God does not do this
Story without us. He is making all things new, and His Story
is powerful because He makes all things new through His
reborn creations. Just as sin came through one man (Adam)
and impacted us all, righteousness comes through one man
(Jesus) as well. Sin is contagious, but so is righteousness.
God desires to radically change hearts in order to promote
His Story.

Micah 6:8 tells us what God wants from us: "*To do justice, to love kindness and to walk humbly with your God.*"
When it comes to God's justice, grace, and mercy, we want
to be right under the faucet. We want these gifts to pour into
our lives and fill us up. God, however, is asking us to *be*
the faucet. He wants us to be the conduit through which the
world sees His justice, His grace, and His mercy. The fruit
is not for the sake of the tree. The purpose of the fruit is to
heal the nations.

Apart from God's people, there is no justice, no agape
love, no true joy, and definitely no peace. If we long for
peace on earth then God's people must abide in the Vine.
Patience, kindness, gentleness, faithfulness, and self-control
do not manifest in a disconnected branch. The world desperately needs the fruit of the Spirit, and this fruit only comes
through abiding.

The Book of Genesis gives us an amazing example of
a life lived this way. Joseph was the youngest and favorite

of the twelve sons of Jacob. Joseph dreamed that his older brothers would bow down to him. His brothers, not liking this at all, sold him into slavery and lied to their father that Joseph had been killed. For the next thirteen years, Joseph suffered in slavery and prison. And yet, he abided in God. Joseph remained faithful to God, trusting Him to take care of everything. Finally one day Joseph, the Dreamer, was able to interpret the dreams of the Pharaoh. He prepared the world for a famine that would have eliminated most of the human race. He understood and acted within the wisdom of God to prevent the destruction of the then-known world.

When his family came looking for grain, not realizing that Joseph was their brother, Joseph did not reveal himself immediately, but instead tested his brothers' hearts. Finally, unable to keep his secret any longer, he revealed his true identity and reunited with his family. As his brothers begged for mercy, Joseph said, *"But don't feel badly, don't blame yourselves for selling me. God was behind it. God sent me here ahead of you to save lives"* (Genesis 45:5, *The Message*).

Joseph went through all his suffering to save lives. What benefit was Joseph's imprisonment for Joseph? What was the pay-off for him? He missed more than twenty years with his family. He was falsely accused, imprisoned, and abandoned for years. His individual story was hard, but in the context of God's Story, Joseph's faithfulness to God saved nations. God's people would have died. There would be no Moses, no Law, no Prophets, and no Old Testament. There would be no Jews, no Messiah, and no Christians. Joseph's faithfulness in a lonely prison cell is why you and I are here reading this book. Maybe, just maybe, the seemingly intolerable suffering in your life and mine has more significance than we know. Our individual stories alone are sad. Caught up in God's Story, however, our lives make a momentous difference. God is using our abiding suffering to produce an amazing harvest. There is no "Plan B."

ABIDING IN CHRIST

To live the abundant life is to stop striving to survive the day-to-day. This life is not about material things or happiness, the fodder of the commonplace. When Jesus spoke about giving us abundant life, He was offering us the ability to abundantly produce fruit. Not just any fruit, but fruit that will last. This abundance does not come to us but rather flows through us. In order to experience this life, we must learn how to breathe in God's presence and breathe out our fallen coping strategies. We must learn to abide in the Vine as we heal together with Him.

When we seek Him first, and His righteousness, everything else is attended to (Matthew 6:33). When we pray according to His will, He hears us (1 John 5:14). When we are abiding in Him, we are surrendered to His will. Our prayers are no longer about advancing our stories but about progressing God's Story, which transcends and heals ours. To abide in Christ is to live fully in God's Story as it renews, restores, and remakes our lives into something abundantly fruitful. When we are truly abiding, what we know in our heads and experience in our hearts begin to match. The facts and the truth go together. We know the truth, and we know the Truth. We find the wholeness we crave when we connect, own, and surrender as a way of life.

Going Deeper

1. As a disciple of Jesus, have you moved from following Him to abiding in Him? If so, how has your life changed?
2. Jesus has a matching wound for yours. What hurt do you want to offer Him for healing?

3. Which "fruit substitutes" do you see in your own heart?

4. So often the pursuit of happiness is the central focus of our lives. It is the American Dream. How does this relentless pursuit get in the way of the abundant life?

5. How difficult is it for you to abide, stay, remain in Christ? What pulls you away?

6. Your story is critical to God's Story as God's Story is critical in yours. Describe a scene in your story where you were aware of God's presence working through your unique life for His Storyline.

7. Can you relate to Joseph? How is your story similar to his?

# 11

# Just Breathe:
## *Living Abundantly*

*"If you obey the Spirit of God and practice in your physical life all that God has put in your heart by His Spirit, when the crisis comes you will find your nature will stand by you." Oswald Chambers*

*"Go confidently in the direction of your dreams. Live the life you've imagined." Thoreau*

*"I dwell in possibility." Emily Dickenson*

Christianity is unique from every other world religion. Everyone else believes we must do something in order to reach God. Christianity states that we could do nothing to save ourselves, and so God reached out to us. Other religions teach that we either are gods or that we become gods. Christianity teaches that God became man. They believe in earning. We believe in receiving. They put their trust in their goodness. We put our trust in God's goodness.

When we are trying to earn our right standing with God, we are acting as though we practice another world religion. This is not how the Christian faith works. When we try to use formulas to "get God to answer" in the way we want

Him to respond, we are acting like members of other religions, not Christians. When we are our own source for how life works, we are choosing another path that will not lead us to the abundant life. The Bible talks about this "version" of the Christian life as being "under the Law." We want to know our part that triggers God to do His part. While God will always do His part, it is not a formula. It is a relationship. It is an inhale and exhale motion of surrender, trusting God with all we own, trusting Yahweh with the outcome of our situation, trusting I Am with the most vulnerable parts of our hearts. This is Biblical faith. It is the foundation of how everything happens in the abundant life.

## TRANSPOSING

Any musician will tell you that transposing a song is when you perform the same song in a different key. We change keys because it may be easier to play or to sing in another scale. But the essence of the song is exactly the same. To the untrained ear, if a song is played in the key of C Major, and twenty minutes later is played again in the key of F Major, we would recognize the same song was played but we would not necessarily catch the change in pitch.

The same song in a different key.

We often think of the abundant life in these terms. Instead of a new life, we approach God's offering of salvation and transformation as though it requires us to do our same life but in the key of Jesus. Instead of something radically new, we think of the Christian life as basically cleaning up the old.

For the most part, our lives do stay much the same. We keep the same families, the same jobs, and the same houses. These things do not necessarily change because we have come to follow Christ. Yes, we have a new perspective on sin and grace and church attendance and Bible study. But there is something deeper that must be changed. Rather than attempt to "Christianize" the old ways of thinking, we need a new way. Since the core of the Gospel is our oneness relationship with God, we need a new perspective on relationships. Tim Keller, pastor of Redeemer Presbyterian Church in New York City, points out our consumer mindset toward relationships. As fallen people, our basic motivation is self-preservation, leaving us with a consumer approach as we relate to others.

If I need to buy pencils then I want the best deal. If I find a very nice pencil salesman who offers me a good price for the quality that I seek, we have an arrangement, a relationship. If, however, I meet another pencil person who can get me a better price for the quality and quantity I need, I will move on. Regardless of the relationship I develop with the first pencil salesman, I will abandon it for a more profitable relationship for me. It's not personal; it's business.

Our fallen mindset is the same in interpersonal relationships with others and with God. We are in love as long as the other gives us good feelings and meets our needs. How many affairs happen because we think someone else may meet our needs more effectively but at less cost to us? Hiding behind the excuse that "we fell out of love" people move on until the new relationship dies as well.

Friendships fall apart when encounters together lose energy and purpose. With no immediate pay-off for the time together, friendships drift and dissolve, fading quietly into "we used to be friends."

We also drift in our relationship with God. We think since Jesus died on the cross the rest is up to us. We depend on Him for salvation and for finding our lost keys. But we are consumers. We like quick results, speedy response times, and the least effort on our part. When we call 911 we expect an instant fix. When we cry out to God, we sometimes don't hear from Him on the matter for months, even years. Or He asks us to do seemingly unrelated or unnecessary things, like forgive others, so we lean into our own wisdom instead of trusting His. His results take too long or are not what we want so we do it ourselves. As Christian consumers, we are offering God the opportunity to give us the best deal before we try something else. But the moment-to-moment reactions, impulses, and feelings must be surrendered in the moments they happen.

The old life transposed is a life of striving to overcome sin. The old self is prone to isolation, addictions, passivity, entitlement, and independence. It is the part of us that must be crucified with Christ because God is offering so much more. The abundant life is not about cleaning up, or transposing, the old life into something "Christian." The abundant life is a transformed life that does not view God as a resource but instead views him as *the* Source.

While transposing a song does not take much time, it is still the same song. Transposing our lives does not take much time either, but they are still the same lives. Jesus called those who transposed their lives "whitewashed tombs." While they looked clean on the outside, the inside was still dead.

## TRANSFORMATION

*And do not be conformed to this world, but be transformed by the renewing of your mind, so that you may prove what the will of God is, that which is good and acceptable and perfect (Romans 12:2).*

The word "transformation" here is the Greek word μεταμορφόω, from which we get our word metamorphosis. It means to change into another form. For most of us, we think of butterflies changing from caterpillars or acorns becoming oak trees. We think of a process not an instant result. We think of something new from something other. We think of something different from when it started.

If I plant an acorn to grow an oak tree, the seed will die after it is put in the soil. By die, I mean the hard outer shell will break off, and it will no longer be a seed. The acorn comes with the entire blueprint for a tree buried inside its DNA. As an acorn, it looks nothing like an oak tree. But it will if it dies.

After the seed dies, it begins to change. Sprouts begin to form and the rooting begins. This process takes time and is not seen from the surface. As the roots grow larger and go deeper, there is still no evidence to the naked eye that anything has happened. Finally, the stem breaks through the dirt and we have proof that an acorn was planted there. It takes awhile to see the results, and it will take longer still before we have a strong, healthy tree.

Our transformation is like this. As we are planted in God's Story, our old selves die. The parts of us that isolate, control, demand, attack, and flee must cease. They are survival techniques that don't die easily. But we must offer ourselves, again and again, as living sacrifices. As we do this, the blueprint within begins to do its work. Created in God's image, for relationship with Him, we begin to root in God's Story. While we are often unable to see that God is doing anything, He is rooting us deeper and making us stronger so that by the time our new lives begin to surface, we will be able to withstand any storm that comes. Don't rush Him and don't worry. If you have given your life to God, He will finish what He has started. He may be rooting you right now. But He does this to protect you later. Without strong roots, a tree will easily fall. Without this time of unseen transformation, we will fall as well. So what is our part? We connect, we own, and we surrender. As we do this, God does something that only God can do: He transforms us into His own likeness.

As we explore the choice of words Paul used in his letter to the Romans, we find that he speaks in the passive voice throughout the verse. Don't *be* conformed but *be* transformed. In other words conforming and transforming happen to us, they are not actions that originate with us. Paul warns that there are forces at work that are constantly moving in our direction. As we live within the context of time, on Planet Earth, life is always changing and progressing in some direction.

Imagine a swiftly moving river as it approaches a fork. As we sit in our canoe we can steer which way we will head, but we cannot stop. We also cannot determine the outcome of the direction we pick. All we can do is lean one way or the other and accept whatever comes with the path of our choice. We can be conformed to the world or we can be transformed into the likeness of Christ. There is no other alternative. If we choose to conform, all we need to do is float. The current will automatically take us there. This is the wide road, the common choice. When we encounter the struggles of life, both large and small, we will automatically choose to lean toward our own resources. We will elect to protect ourselves by calling forth whatever learned means we have always depended on for help. Conforming looks like isolation, addictions, passivity, entitlement, and independence. Relationships are the means to our end. People help us or they don't. We take on the role of wise consumer as we strategize how much we give compared to how much we are given.

This sounds harsh, but it is subtle. We are not trying to be consumers. We want to give from our hearts with generosity and grace. But we do not naturally float to self-sacrifice. We can't. If we are our own source for what we need (without God), we cannot give what we do not have. We cannot purely offer the fruit of love if the Vine has not produced it in us. What we offer without the Vine is our own version of love attached to dozens of strings that bring a pay-off for us. We give to get because we have to.

The transformation process, the other prong in the fork of this river, requires that we lean in the direction of a renewed mind. This is the narrow path, the road less traveled. We lean by accepting God's invitation to change. Jesus stands at the fork of this rapidly moving river and invites us to connect with Him, own what we want to change, and surrender it to Him for transformation. We can be conformed and look more and more like consumers, or we can be transformed and look more and more like Jesus. We do not strive to be transformed any more than a branch strives to bear fruit. Remaining, pressing in, not pulling apart, and residing in the Truth is how we are transformed.

Transformation is a miracle as great as salvation. In essence, God promises that if I am a wild branch that grew from a thorn bush and I am engrafted into a grape vine, I will begin to produce grapes. Born into sin from my mother's womb, now engrafted into the Vine, I produce the fruit of the Spirit. How does this happen?

- How does a baby know how to take his first breath?
- How did the Red Sea part?
- How was the leper healed?
- How does a humming bird fly?
- How were Abraham and Sarah able to conceive Isaac?
- How does the Earth know to keep spinning?
- How was Joseph able to accurately interpret the Pharaoh's dreams and save the then-known world?
- How was Jesus raised from the dead?

I don't know. But I do know the same power is behind them all. Within this power, God is making all things new. If He can keep the Earth spinning, He can change you and me. He does not simply clean up the old self, dust it off, and tolerate its repulsiveness. He does not excuse us as "only human" and overlook our shortcomings because we can't help it. He does not demand that we become better people or even "good Christians." He does not expect us to sing our old song in the key of Jesus. He wants to save that precious, Image-bearing, true self in us all, stripping away the trappings and snares of the world, and setting us free to enjoy Him forever. His Story is that good.

## GOD'S STORY

And so we end where we began. God is making all things new. But He's not doing it through efficiency and goals. God is restoring through relationships, the very place that Adam and Eve fell. God heals through submission of Himself to us as we submit ourselves to Him. He is not pulling us from our circumstances or keeping all the bad things from happening. He is saving us by bearing up under the weight of our sin as we react to those bad circumstances. And He asks us to connect with Him as He carries it for us. As we do, we experience His rich, deep love for us, and we don't want to sin anymore. The essence of who we are changes.

We have seen people who live this and they inspire us to continue to believe. They are our own personal Hebrews 11 heroes of faith. By this kind of faith, we see the single mom who is devastated by her ex-husband's affair but still prays for him. As she prays, she trusts that God has heard her and it is now in His hands. She is telling her son that God is in control no matter what happens to them.

By faith, my pastor friend in India loves God so much that he and his eight children are ready to die for Jesus. His oldest son knows to take half the family in the opposite direction if they are attacked, so that at least part of the family can continue the ministry.

By faith, families surviving the suicide of loved ones trust God's goodness to get them through. By faith, I've seen those who have been left financially devastated and horribly abandoned in this way refuse to allow bitterness and unforgiveness to build in their hearts.

Similarly, my prison chaplain friends in Rwanda daily serve the very people who killed their families in the genocide of 1994. Refusing to disobey God in revenge or hatred, they love those who have taken the most precious people from their lives.

By faith, a husband transforms from dominating during conflict to looking at such moments as opportunities to surrender and do the right thing, learning how to submit power rather than use it as a weapon. He is demonstrating what makes men great.

By faith, another husband overcomes issues with pornography because of a wife that loves him unconditionally. While devastated by his behavior, she refuses to shame him for it. Because of her surrendered heart, he experiences the unconditional love of God for the first time. Safe to finally break, he is able to surrender his own heart for healing. I have seen it happen more than once.

I could tell of the many mentally ill people I know who trust God for every provision. Unable to function without Him, He honors their surrendered hearts and gives them quality lives.

These are people we know, in every day life, of whom the world is not worthy. Their circumstances are not easy and their pain has been deep. But they have learned to connect with God, own what is theirs, surrender it to Him, and receive what He is offering in return. They are living out the abundant life on a daily basis.

If you are a Christ-follower, we know how your story will end. But how will your story be remembered? Will you be known as accomplished or connected? Are you a speck remover or a log remover? Will you be remembered as efficient or surrendered? When your story is summed up in a paragraph, will it start with, "By faith …"?

God is offering us the abundant life right now. To prove it, He sent His Son, crushed Him for our sins, raised Him from the dead, and sent His Holy Spirit to finish the job in our hearts. All He is asking us to do is connect, own, and surrender.

## Going Deeper

1. What areas of your life are "under the law" that you are still trying to fix yourself?
2. In what ways have you been taught to "transpose" your life?
3. As you allow God to transform you, what parts of your old life still need to die?
4. Have you ever been in a season of "rooting"? What was it like?
5. Conforming is easier than transforming. What pulls you to conform and what draws you toward transformation?
6. Who would you add to your "Hebrews 11" list?
7. Complete this sentence: "By faith, (*your name*), ...

www.abidingnotstriving.com